Learn Like a Polymath:

How to Teach Yourself Anything, Develop Multidisciplinary Expertise, and Become Irreplaceable

By Peter Hollins,
Author and Researcher at
petehollins.com

Table of Contents

Chapter 1. Deconstructing the Polymath

Think of the smartest, most successful people history has ever known. Which names come to your mind? Be it Einstein, Da Vinci, Bill Gates, Isaac Newton, Jeff Bezos, Elon Musk, or someone like them, their success can be attributed to one common factor: they were all polymaths. This means that they specialized and were knowledgeable in several different domains, and they integrated these disparate fields of study to create art, come up with scientific inventions, and so on.

Though this might sound intimidating and only achievable for those who are naturally highly intelligent, anyone can become a polymath with the right mindset and attitude. You may have heard that it's better to specialize or master one skill rather than be a jack of all trades. Some cultures even have sayings like "a man with twelve talents has nothing to eat for dinner." However, the modern workplace increasingly requires a more diversified skill set in order to thrive and achieve success.

To be the best in the world at one thing, you need to be better than everyone else who specializes in that field. But to be great, without being the best, at three or more subjects simultaneously is not only rare, but also significantly easier than being the greatest of the great in one field.

As such, being a polymath can be critical to leading a successful professional life, and in this book, we're going to discuss how you can start thinking like one too.

Two Paths to Polymathy

Over the years, several theories have been presented to explain what makes someone a polymath. One such theory is Howard Gardner's notion of multiple intelligences. To understand this theory, we first need to delve into what the traditional view of intelligence has been.

Historically, intelligence has been perceived in fairly one-dimensional ways. Your intellectual capacity was thought to be fixed at birth as a result of your genetic inheritance, without any possibility of change in the future. This intelligence mainly consisted of one's ability to comprehend language and logic, which could be measured using some standardized tests, such as IQ tests. (LumenLearning, Keith 2009)

Since then, much progress has been made in broadening our concept of intelligence. Gardner, a Harvard psychologist, considered the traditional view of intelligence insufficient for explaining how different people learn and exhibit their smarts. Where those who are highly articulate or able to solve complex logical problems are often considered to be conventionally intelligent, he emphasized those who are gifted in more creative fields, such as architecture, music, and dance.

Those who excel in creative fields rather than logical ones are often labeled as "learning disabled," thought to be suffering from ADD, or are simply cast off as underachievers. This is because most classrooms cannot accommodate the ways of learning these individuals need to become more proficient in different subjects, and as a result, these learners don't excel in areas they are actually quite capable of grasping. Gardner's theory revolutionizes this outdated approach to intelligence.

So what is his theory of multiple intelligences all about? According to Gardner, we all possess at least seven unique forms of intelligence through which we learn and retain information. All of these types of intelligence can be cultivated with the right learning tools, although some individuals are more developed in certain forms of intelligence compared to others.

His system outlines the following different types of intelligence:

Linguistic intelligence

Individuals with high levels of linguistic intelligence are generally articulate and adept at expressing themselves through spoken or written words. They find it easy to learn new languages, enjoy reading various kinds of literature, playing word games or debating, and generally have a unique way with words. Such individuals commonly take up lawyering, writing, public speaking, journalism, and other language-related jobs.

Logical-mathematical intelligence

People who possess logical-mathematical intelligence are attuned to logical thinking and have excellent powers of reasoning or deduction. They are good at thinking abstractly about problems that involve various concepts or numbers, which makes them temperamentally suited to maths and the natural sciences. These skills are useful for those involved in programming, scientific research, accountancy, etc.

Spatial intelligence

Spatially intelligent individuals are great at visualizing information and processing or manipulating it in critically evaluative ways. This is similar to logical-mathematical intelligence, except spatial intelligence usually involves physical spaces or environments and the objects placed within them. Architects, painters, and engineers are some examples of people with high spatial intelligence.

Bodily-Kinesthetic intelligence

Having bodily-kinesthetic intelligence means possessing the ability to use your body and physical movements to retain information. People who have successfully developed this type of intelligence prefer to learn in a more hands-on fashion that involves dynamic activity rather than excessive thinking. They are also good at expressing themselves through their body language. Athletes, gym instructors, dancers, and actors are all intelligent in this way.

Musical intelligence

Musically intelligent individuals learn through sounds, rhythms, patterns, beats, and tones. Their talent lies in being able to produce, perform, and appreciate music. Conductors, songwriters, music teachers, instrumentalists and singers possess this type of intelligence in abundance.

Interpersonal intelligence

Interpersonal intelligence involves having a keen awareness and sensitivity to the emotions, mental states, and desires of other people. These individuals are conventionally known as "people smart" and can hit it off with just about anyone they meet. Interpersonally intelligent people tend to have many friends, learn through their interactions with others, and are generally empathetic in nature. This type of intelligence is common among psychologists, salesmen, politicians, etc.

Intrapersonal intelligence

This form of intelligence is the opposite of the previous one in that it involves being deeply aware of your own spiritual, mental, and emotional self. Individuals who possess intrapersonal intelligence are deeply aware of their strengths and weaknesses, fears, motivations, desires, and capacities. Counselors, social workers, and philosophers are generally high in intrapersonal intelligence. (LumenLearning, Keith 2009) (SimplyPsychology, Marenus 2020)

While these are the seven main categories of intelligence in Gardner's system, he would later go on to add three more: naturalist, existentialist, and spiritual intelligence. Though existential and spiritual intelligences in particular have received much attention recently, Gardner claims that these types are qualitatively different from the original seven laid out above.

As the names suggest, naturalist intelligence involves being able to distinguish between nuances inherent to plants, weather patterns, animals, and other natural phenomena. Existentially intelligent people are proficient at tackling life's deepest questions, such as why we exist, whether God exists, and so on. Lastly, spiritual intelligence is the ability to place one's actions and life within a broader context in meaningful ways that give us direction and inspire us to action. (LumenLearning, Keith 2009)

Now that we've laid out what kinds of intelligence exist, we come to how these categories relate to becoming a polymath. By one possible view, being a polymath involves becoming proficient in at least three of these multiple intelligences. For example, a counselor may treat his or her patients effectively through their interpersonal intelligence. However, to be a polymath who excels in this field, they may also want to develop their linguistic, intrapersonal, and logical-mathematical intelligences.

Similarly, an artist might well be high in spatial or musical intelligence, but developing their interpersonal, linguistic, and intrapersonal intelligences might help them achieve greater success than what they would have managed by just being good at art.

Adherents of this view hold that increasing your skills or knowledge can primarily be done in a compartmentalized fashion, wherein training your various intelligences one by one helps one achieve polymathy. For detractors, It's unclear how distinct these intelligences really are, or whether science shows that they actually exist. Nonetheless, Gardner's ideas remain an influential theory that is particularly popular among educators. Besides this, there is another prominent view of what makes a polymath, and this perspective is described in the next section.

This next view of what makes a polymath has some things in common with both the traditional view of intelligence as well as Gardner's multiple intelligences. We'll refer to it as the biological view of intelligence, since it is heavily dependent on the structure and development of your brain. The human brain is one of the most complex organs in our entire body, with close to 100 billion neurons and 100 trillion connections all interacting with each other to coordinate our daily functions.

Different parts of our brain are responsible for managing their own separate functions, and being a polymath requires these parts to be well developed individually, as well as in connection to the whole. As you'll see, one part of your brain is responsible for logical thinking, while another controls your ability to interpret language.

According to the biological view of intelligence, to become a polymath, you need a brain whose distinct parts are developed beyond the average in ways that facilitate higher order logical or linguistic intelligence. To find out more about this theory, read on.

You might have come across the notion of some people being left-brained whereas others are right-brained. If you're the kind of person who is methodical and always thinking rationally, you fit into the former camp, whereas more artistically oriented individuals fall into the latter category. (Healthline, Weatherspoon 2019)

This theory is partly based on the way scientists have formulated the function of specific parts of our brain. To understand this in greater depth, we need to familiarize ourselves with some basics on brain biology.

Our brains consist of three overarching parts: the cerebrum, the cerebellum, and the brain stem. The cerebrum is divided into two hemispheres, which control processes like movement, speech, hearing, vision, regulation of emotions, reasoning capabilities, etc. Each hemisphere is then divided into four lobes, which individually perform the aforementioned, along with other functions. These are called the frontal, temporal, occipital, and parietal lobes. (Healthline, Seladi-Schulman, 2018)

The frontal lobe can be found in the forward region of our head and is responsible for many essential functions of our brain. This includes emotional regulation, reasoning, planning, and most importantly, determining our personality. Its role in controlling the way we express ourselves, memory, language, impulse control, sexual behaviors, and more makes it central to the way others perceive us.

The temporal lobe, located on the sides of our head near our ears, is primarily engaged in two distinct roles. The first role is controlling visual memory, which helps you remember people's faces, objects, etc. The second is managing your verbal memory, which helps you interpret language and speech. Besides these functions, the temporal lobe also plays a part in the formation of long-term memories and the retention of smells.

The parietal lobe is largely responsible for our spatial intelligence. Moreover, it also plays a role in interpreting sense data that is related to vision, hearing, pain, and other sensations. The parietal lobe combines all the various inputs it receives from our senses to facilitate cognition and thinking. (KenHub, Shahid, 2020)

Lastly, the occipital lobes, which can be found at the back of your head, are mainly responsible for processing visual information. This includes colors, shapes, lighting, etc.

As you can see, these four lobes that together make up the cerebrum are involved in functions related to interpreting various forms of sensory input to allow for our cognitive processes. However, the cerebellum and brainstem, the two other main parts of the brain, are also significant for our routine functioning.

The cerebellum can be found below the cerebrum and is crucial in coordinating operations that are related to physical movement. It helps us maintain our posture and balance while walking, allows motor functions such as riding a bicycle, and facilitates motor learning-related activities like learning how to play an instrument. It also plays a part in regulating our speech. (MedicalNewsToday, Fisher 2018)

While the cerebellum makes many of our voluntary movements possible, the brain stem is in charge of controlling our involuntary processes. This includes our breathing, regulation of our heartbeat, sleep and eating cycles, sensitivity to pain, etc. The brain stem is particularly important because all information to the cerebrum and cerebellum passes through it first, making any damage to it the most catastrophic of any part of our brain. (KenHub, Crumbie, 2020)

You would be forgiven for thinking that you have mistakenly stumbled across a biology textbook, but this information is essential to our purpose—the distribution of functions across different parts of our brain might tell us something important about being a polymath. If we were to reject Gardner's multiple intelligences as being the root of polymathic abilities in favor of this biological view, a polymath would be someone with a well-developed brain with a particularly advanced cerebrum.

We know that the brains of intelligent people have more folds in them, which increases their surface area and allows for a higher density of neurons overall. Thus, if specific parts of your brain, such as the frontal lobe or the parietal lobe, were to have a higher number of folds, that might explain the source of polymathic ability. The former being denser would point to improved reasoning skills, which the latter could indicate heightened linguistic abilities.

One might be tempted to accept this proposition given that Gardner's theory appears more abstract, while the biological view seems more scientifically grounded and thus reliable.

Alternatively, we could also combine the two theories to understand what it takes to become a polymath. A person with high spatial intelligence might just be someone whose parietal lobes have matured extensively. Similarly, an individual who is strong in logical-mathematical intelligence could simply be someone whose frontal lobes have grown beyond what might be considered the average.

This points to a similarity in both theories, which is their delineation of specific functions to either a particular type of intelligence, or a specific part of our brain. However, it's important to note there is a difference between talking about various types of intelligences in a way similar to Gardner, and actually believing these intelligences to exist.

Saying that someone is musically intelligent does not mean that Gardner's idea of musical intelligence exists. Someone could simply be prolific at music composition by virtue of possessing a well-developed brain.

So which is it? Is Gardner right, or does the biological view paint a more accurate picture of what makes a polymath? Or is it a combination of both?

You might be relieved to know that, in truth, both of the preceding theories about polymathic abilities are deeply flawed and fail to do a good job of explaining what makes someone a polymath. It might be tempting to think that polymaths simply have more developed brains than we do, or that they are smarter in ways that we just aren't, but neither of these possibilities is accurate.

While both theories sound perfectly reasonable in their own right, neither has been sufficiently backed by scientific research to be taken seriously. To take Gardner's multiple intelligences, there is nothing to suggest that there are actually distinct "intelligences" at play when individuals show proficiency in a certain field such as music or debate. The types of intelligences as Gardner lays them out are also hard to measure and evaluate. Some, like intrapersonal and interpersonal intelligence, can be hard to define at all.

One factor that makes these barriers significantly worse is that Gardner has refused to outline specific components of each intelligence type or suggest ways in which they can be verified. Instead, he has chosen to simply describe them extensively, which brings his theory on par with any other abstract theory on intelligence. (PsychologyToday, McGreal 2013)

Regardless of these issues, there have been fairly rigorous efforts to prove the validity of his theory. Researchers have improvised and come up with their own guidelines of assessment, but none of these have proven conclusive in establishing Gardner's theory.

The general consensus appears to be that each form of intelligence he highlights has a high degree of correlation with other forms. So if a person has high logical-mathematical intelligence, part of the reason behind that is because they also have high linguistic intelligence. One of Gardner's intelligence types, naturalistic intelligence, was found to be correlated with all seven other types. (PsychologyToday, McGreal 2013)

Despite all its flaws, Gardner's theory does do some things right. It rightly undermines the authority of IQ tests, making it clear that you do not necessarily need a high IQ to be intelligent or a polymath. It also expresses the notion that one isn't intelligent in permanent ways, and that mental abilities can fluctuate with the right approach and tools. This conclusion will be instrumental in our discussion of how to become a polymath, because it suggests that anyone can master a diverse set of skills.

However, these ideas cannot compensate for the fact that ultimately there is very little, if any, scientific research supporting Gardner's theory. Even if there was, being a polymath isn't just about acquiring a ton of knowledge in different domains. You need to be able to use this knowledge in collaborative ways, and there is nothing in Gardner's theory to suggest that someone with, say, intrapersonal, interpersonal, and linguistic intelligence can necessarily use all three together as opposed to individually.

This brings us to the biological view, and why exactly it fails to explain polymathic abilities. Many of the criticisms of this approach are similar in structure to the critique of Gardner's theory, namely because both seek to isolate functions and types of intelligence in ways that are not scientifically useful in understanding intelligence.

The claim that certain parts of our brain exclusively handle certain functions is simply misleading, and one can see this even by knowing the very basics of what roles various parts of our brain play. There is great overlap between, say, the way different lobes contribute to the interpretation of sense data.

A great example of this is when we listen to music. Based on the descriptions of what each lobe in our brain does, you might think that music is primarily interpreted through our temporal or parietal lobe since these sections process auditory information. However, not only does listening to music require different regions in both of these lobes that are responsible for separate functions, but it also involves the frontal lobe and even the cerebellum. As such, listening to music, like so many other activities, requires almost all of our brain.

Another reason the biological view fails is that we exert very little control over how different parts of our brain develop. Ninety percent of our brains develop before the age of five. (Brown, Jernigan 2012) If someone wanted to be a polymath based on this view, they would be placing an undue burden on factors like upbringing, culture, etc., in shaping our abilities.

From a biological perspective, there would be no way for one to "acquire" polymathic abilities since that would be entirely contingent on external considerations. This lends credence to the fallacy wherein intelligent people are smart just because they won the genetic lottery, and there is no scope for improvement for those who didn't luck out. Thankfully, we know these claims to be false, and one can indeed "become" a polymath.

All of these points, when considered together, make a damning case against the biological view of polymathy. Consequently, the theory of left and right brains becomes highly suspect as well. This theory is another way of saying that particular parts of our brain are responsible for specific functions. What makes these theories so appealing is that they appear to give us greater insight into who we are, or why we aren't who we want to be. If you're good at math, it's because you're left brained, and if you're good at composing music, then it's your right brain dominance expressing itself.

While these explanations are attractive for their simplicity, things are never quite this straightforward. There is a complex web of biological factors that make someone more attuned to logical thinking versus artistic expression. Like in the case of listening to music, both of them involve different parts of the brain all working together.

This brings us to the fundamental truth about being and becoming a polymath: you don't need to be intelligent in specific ways or have a certain level of brain development to achieve polymathic abilities. Anyone can become a polymath through the tools and ideas expressed in this book, no matter who you are or what your general intelligence level.

Cross-Pollination as the Key

If you want to become a polymath, there are two things you need in abundance: a willingness to learn new and different things, along with the time and effort that goes into learning them. There is nothing inherently special about polymaths; they have simply taken the time to learn the things they wanted to be good at.

In some ways, learning is a skill in itself. Acquiring new skills requires discipline and unwavering focus, especially when the thing you're trying to learn is challenging or alien to your knowledge base. The fact that we're constantly being told to specialize instead of generalizing our skill set makes it easier and more tempting to abandon our efforts at diversifying our areas of expertise. Warnings against being a generalist have been made for several hundreds of years, with Shakespeare receiving one of the first.

Several cultures have their own sayings that illustrate this warning too. In Eastern Europe, for example, one reads, "Seven trades, the eighth one—poverty." While these beliefs may have been relevant at a certain period of time, our modern era is one where change is constant and rapid. We need to arm ourselves with multiple useful skills to stay relevant and retain value in an increasingly competitive economic world, no matter what it is that we do.

This brings us to a concept that is becoming increasingly relevant in the business world: cross-pollination. Ordinarily, cross-pollination refers to pollen from one type of crop mixing with crops of another type, resulting in the creation of hybrids. This is often done intentionally to create all sorts of unique combinations.

The same concept is applied to business, wherein acquiring expertise in disciplines or skills that are unrelated to each other results in uniquely qualified candidates who think in creative and productive ways. This perception has also been backed by several studies in recent times.

One report by Lee Fleming in Harvard Business Review examined 17,000 patents and found that innovators with qualifications in disparate fields were less likely to produce financially viable ideas than their counterparts. However, it also found that when these innovators do experience a creative breakthrough, the result is of "unusually high value—superior to the best innovations achieved by conventional approaches."

Another study by Brian Uzzi, a professor at Northwestern University, analyzed more than 26 million scientific research papers dating hundreds of years apart. He found that the papers which ended up being most influential were composed by teams made up of people with diverse backgrounds.

A third enquiry by David Epstein in his book *Range* has revealed that influential scientists are much more likely to have diverse interests outside of their primary area of research than the average scientist.

Lastly, the investigations of Robert Root-Bernstein and Michele Marie Root Bernstein have established that the more artistic interests scientists hold, the more likely they are to gain eminence in their field. These scientists noticeably integrated skills they had acquired through their artistic interests, be it visual arts or music, into their professional scientific work. This made them more likely to be cited and receive prestigious awards like the Nobel Prize.

These studies are just the tip of the iceberg given the amount of research that has been done on the correlation between polymathy and success. All of these make a very strong case for diversifying your skill set given the advantages it's been shown to have instead of specializing in one trade alone. However, there is one more study that will be crucial to our understanding of what exactly a polymath is and how you can become one.

Michael Araki is one of the few theorists who has attempted to create a system that exactly describes what components go into being a polymath. Generally, the word *polymath* refers to someone who is intellectually oriented, or someone who is simply good at many different things, and even as an ideal that should be pursued but can never actually be reached.

The problem with definitions like these is that they don't illustrate degrees well. Exactly how intellectually bent does a polymath need to be? How many different things do I need to be good at, and how can I measure how good I am at those things? Problems like these can make achieving the goal of polymathy harder, but Araki poses a neat solution to them.

According to Araki, there are three main components of being a polymath: breadth, depth, and integration.

Breadth is the largest category of the three, and consists of the knowledge you have of different subjects or skills. Often this is considered to be the only important component of polymathy, but Araki warns against making such an inference. Breadth only includes the superficial knowledge you have of certain areas. So if you've slightly familiar with Freudian theory, your knowledge of psychology along with other areas of interest forms a part of your breadth.

Depth refers to the vertical accumulation of knowledge in specific fields. This, combined with breadth, makes up the store of your total knowledge across various disciplines and topics. However, these two factors aren't enough to make you a polymath. You could be incredibly knowledgeable about psychology, philosophy, and political theory, but that doesn't necessarily mean you're adept at using your knowledge in one field across the others.

This is where integration comes in. The final piece of the polymath puzzle rests in your ability to connect, articulate, and synthesize disparate disciplines together to be creative in novel ways. This combination of depth, breadth, and integration is very similar to the cross-pollination theory outlined above. The latter involves taking two divergent types of pollen and bringing them together to create something altogether new, and that's exactly what Araki's theory of polymathy states.

You take at least three different, disparate disciplines or skills, get to know them sufficiently well, and combine them instead of using individual skills separately. To take the example of Leonardo da Vinci, he wouldn't be a polymath if he were just good at drawing, efficient at doing math, and possessed the ability to invent things. He's considered a polymath because he used mathematical principles in his artwork, which he in turn employed to come up with inventions. He cross-pollinated (or integrated) his three skills in ways few else have been able to.

Araki's theory of polymathy solves all of the problems we highlighted with alternative definitions earlier. It gives you an idea of how to measure your expertise in a given field and also tells you how skilled you need to be to qualify as a polymath. Both of these functions are served by the integration component.

If you don't know enough about your chosen topics, you will likely fail to integrate them together. Likewise, if you are successful in integrating them, you can safely conclude that you've sufficiently mastered the topics you're trying to integrate.

Guidelines and a Plan

Now that you've familiarized yourself with what a polymath is and how anyone can become one, it's time to put all the concepts to use and formulate actual guidelines for achieving polymathy. These guidelines rely on your ability to cross-pollinate different subjects and then integrate them in efficient and creative ways. Here's how you can do that:

Step 1

Choose the different areas you want to achieve expertise in. You should pick a minimum of three that are sufficiently distinct from each other. For example, learning about Freudian theory and Jungian psychology wouldn't count since they are both subsets of the same subject. Instead choose a combination like psychology, philosophy, and political theory. Even better if these areas or fields have some relevance to your work.

Step 2

Start by establishing some breadth, which involves gaining some superficial knowledge about the areas of interest you've chosen. The citations on Wikipedia pages for your topics are often a great place to start. You can also simply read the first five to ten articles that show up on rudimentary Google searches. At this stage, all you're trying to do is get to know your topics on a basic level.

Step 3

This is where we add some depth, and there are several ways you can do this. Depending on the type of media you prefer, you can approach learning about your topics in different ways. If you prefer reading, look for some books on Amazon.

Alternatively, you can search for introductory, intermediate, and advanced online courses if you prefer a more audio-visual method of learning. If your topics are academic disciplines like in our example, this should be fairly simplistic. However, in some cases you might need to use a combination of different resources like books, podcasts, YouTube, online courses, etc.

Step 4

While performing the previous step, you'll likely discover that your topics of interest are far too broad, and that you need to choose subtopics within them in order to gain a better understanding of the topic as a whole. So you might choose particular fields within philosophy like ethics or metaphysics along with, say, liberalism and totalitarian movements within political theory.

You don't need to learn everything, so pick your subtopics depending on what interests you and focus on them. The more subtopics you choose the better, but at the same time, your choices need to be practical and manageable so that you can complete your studies and master the topics.

Step 5

Now comes the trickiest step, which is integrating everything you've learned together. Let's say you know some Freudian psychology, a little about totalitarian movements, and ethics. One good way to combine all of this is to study the totalitarian governments like the Nazis, their use of psychological repression as a tool to control their citizens and the morality of such tactics. This is close to the way the Frankfurt School investigated phenomena like the rise of the Nazi party.

Depending on which topics you've chosen, the best way to integrate them is to try and find points of convergence. In this example, totalitarian governments are by definition oppressive, and so we look at the psychological ways in which this oppression plays out. Oppression carries with it strong ethical undertones, but who exactly is morally responsible for the rise of the Nazis? Is it Hitler alone, his cabinet, the entire Nazi party, or Germany as a whole? One can always find areas of convergence; you only need to look diligently enough.

Let's consider another example of how you can go about becoming a polymath.

Step 1

Pick another set of three disciplines or skills you want to learn. This time, let's assume that your interests are theology, philosophy, and logic.

Step 2

Familiarize yourself with these three topics individually. Start with the basics. Since you've chosen theology and philosophy, you can study the problem of evil from the latter and the ways God's existence would address that problem. The question here is, if God is supposed to be perfect and completely good, how can he allow evil to exist? Regarding logic, you'd need to study deductive argumentation to be able to assess whether claims related to God and evil are valid, sound, true, false, etc.

Step 3

Once you've developed some breadth, establish depth. Go deeper into the areas of your study. Get to know the two major paradigms of evil, those espoused by Fyodor Dostoevsky and Hannah Arendt. Then dig deeper into the various theological arguments that might help you answer why these forms of evil exist. Lastly, use your enquiries into logic to evaluate the validity of these arguments.

Step 4

We've already completed step four because we chose our subtopics early based on possible connections between these three disparate disciplines. The problem of evil is a major subtopic in both theology and philosophy, while deductive argumentation is one of three methods of arguing for or against a claim.

Step 5

Lastly, integrate these three categories together. Use your knowledge of the three disciplines to ascertain whether there is any way of reconciling the existence of evil and God together based on logic.

As far as the plan goes, you need to think on a broad level as to what you want to accomplish. This is where you make sure that you are spending your time the way you want to. This can be accomplished by following six steps.

First, decide what you want to learn. This seems obvious, but there are better and worse things to spend your time on.

When considering a course of action, you will want to first consider your strengths and weaknesses. Often, whether it's in work or in play, we're better off emphasizing and developing our strengths than we are trying to minimize our failings. After all, no one is going to ask us to do everything, and when we really have trouble, acquiring help from others is always possible. But excellence in one area, or a small group of areas, easily transforms us into experts in our fields, which is a highly desirable place to be. Emphasizing your strengths when you choose what to spend your time on is a good idea. Of course, if you want to learn something totally new, that's also something you can accomplish!

Even if you're only looking to advance your professional skillset, you should still consider what you want to do when choosing a subject to learn or a skill to develop. Career paths are a consideration, but it's even more important to take into account what sorts of activities make you happy and unhappy. You don't want a degree in accounting if you hate numbers, after all, even if it would improve your paycheck. Paths that align with your interests and are emotionally fulfilling are usually more rewarding.

Consider Darlene, who works as a web developer. She wants to have greater control over the processes that occur on her websites, rather than outsourcing for code when she needs it to perform certain functions she can't create herself. Moreover, she wants to be able to manipulate that code and make it from scratch so that she completely understands what's on her pages. Her vision for her learning is to gain knowledge of more types of code so that she can be a more competent, better-rounded web developer.

The second step is analyzing your current skills and experience to spot gaps in knowledge. Where are you lacking compared to your future self? What do you already know and do well? What do you still need to learn? Can other people fill in these gaps in knowledge for you, or do you need to step up to the plate and seek out additional resources? Once you find areas in which you need to improve, you will be able to discern specific topics you can study and skills you should develop to come closer to your goals. This gives your plan a concrete shape, because you will know exactly what you are missing to get to Point B.

Darlene already develops web pages for a living and knows the most current versions of HTML and CSS by heart, but she currently outsources certain types of coding to others. This leads to problems with version control and gives her a sense of powerlessness over that aspect of her job. If she wants to fill that gap in her knowledge, she needs to study other languages used on the web. She decides to start with Java, as that's the code she most often interacts with without understanding.

Third, identify the proper solution to your problem/deficiency/goal. This is about surveying your resources. Part of your approach will depend on your temperament. Are you a self-starter, or do you learn better in a classroom setting? Do you need a source of knowledge you can pick up and put down as your schedule allows, or can you afford to set up regular appointments with a teacher to develop a skill? Your schedule, income, and preferences all play a role in determining the right resources to seek and employ.

Lots of learning resources exist in the modern world, from books, journals, webpages, and podcasts, to seminars, work teams, and formal classes, to one-on-one instructional training in formal and informal settings.

When choosing a resource to learn from, it's important to take into account your own learning preferences, but that's only one of many considerations. You must also consider the reputation of your source or teacher, and whether you will gain any formal credentials from studying with a specific teacher or demonstrating competence in a certain field. It's also essential to think about convenience, because a class you can't get to is not useful, no matter how well-regarded the teacher may be. By contrast, solo studying offers no emotional or technical support from others, while a course or a tutoring situation may involve substantial help and oversight from someone else. If this support and community might be valuable in the area you're studying, it could be worth paying for.

Darlene is highly motivated but often pressed for time. She considers community college courses, learning from books and journals, and even hiring a private tutor, but ultimately decides to engage in one of the many online programs to help her develop her skills on her own schedule. These courses won't automatically get her credentials, but she's aware that she could take a skills test to certify herself once she gains skill mastery, and as she will have an immediate use for Java in her current job, she's not worried about being unable to use her new knowledge in the future.

The fourth step is developing your learning blueprint. Once you know what you want to accomplish, you should look for people who have already achieved your goal. These people will serve as a step-by-step guide for how to get to where you want.

If the person is famous or no longer living, you can research their life to figure out how they became who you want to become. If they're not particularly famous or renowned, even better, as you can approach them personally and ask about their road to success. Take note of any struggles, education, or personal relationships they had to overcome or pursue to reach their goals, and try to find ways to mimic this path in your own life. This can give you deeper insight into skills to focus on and paths to pursue once your initial research project is complete.

Darlene sits down and has a conversation with her team supervisor about the best ways to advance her career and land a comparable job to her mentor when the time is right. He tells her about specific skills she'll need to learn and certifications she'll need to complete once she gains the skills she needs. He will tell her about the struggles to expect and how to overcome them. Darlene may ultimately choose a different path, but researching blueprints provides clarity and information.

The fifth step is to develop measurable goals. Your learning goals should be simple, specific, and easy to quantify. You need to set up deadlines where you will measure yourself against your expected progress using the metrics you devised, and you need to stick to that schedule. Placing your goals in a public, visible space will increase accountability by ensuring that others are aware of your project and your expectations. Remember, you should be acquiring specific, measurable skills and abilities by set points in time, and these benchmarks should all be in service of your larger learning goal.

If you've chosen a more formal environment, your class times may be set for you, but you must still set aside time to study, learn, and practice on your own. No class gives you all the practice you need to master its skillset on the teacher's time. If you're engaging in self-study, setting up a consistent schedule for studying on your own is even more essential.

Keep in mind, genuinely mastering a skill takes a little time even with the best techniques, so be generous in the study windows you provide yourself. You don't only want time to read or watch a video, but also to reflect upon what you've learned, perform meaningful exercises, and catch and correct the errors you are inevitably going to make.

Darlene marks a schedule for herself based on the units offered in her online course, sets aside specific times to undertake each course, and allot blocks of time to study each unit. She also allocates a specific time each week to take the unit's quiz. She programs all this into her phone so that she doesn't forget the plan, and prints a copy of her calendar to put on her cubicle wall. She stays on track throughout the months, and as a result, she will reach her goal of achieving programming proficiency.

Sixth, set aside time throughout the process to reflect on what you're learning and reevaluate whether you're progressing at your maximum capacity. After all, if one method isn't working, that doesn't mean you're hopeless! Sometimes all you need is more accountability or greater independence to really shine. You want a learning plan that gets your skills where you want them to be, not something that isn't clicking and is therefore wasting your time. A chef will always taste their food while they are making it; you should assess your progress in a similar way.

Darlene sticks diligently to her plan and is happy with her progress, but finds the course itself a little low on support for her needs. She solves this problem by approaching her supervisor with questions when she needs further clarification. He's happy to help her along. Ultimately, she gains the skills she needs and becomes a more efficient, more skilled employee.

Takeaways

- We're often told in different ways that the key to success is specialization, and that being a generalist is inadvisable. Yet, many of the smartest individuals that have ever graced the earth are renowned for being polymaths with skills across multiple subjects.
- The modern workplace and companies are increasingly reliant on polymathic individuals to bring them success, making it imperative for us to diversify our skill set instead of simply mastering one trade and sticking to it.
- But what exactly is a polymath? Howard Gardner's theory of multiple intelligences might be useful in

answering this question. He lays out seven different intelligences that include musical, spatial, linguistic, and other abilities that we all possess. A polymath is simply someone who has developed three or more of these intelligences.

- Alternatively, we have the biological view of polymathy. According to this perspective, different parts of our brain are responsible for their own unique functions. Our ability to write is dictated by one part of our cerebrum, while the capacity to comprehend writing is controlled by another part. A polymath is someone with an exceptionally developed brain whose cerebral lobes have matured beyond the average.

- So which of the two is accurate? The truth is that both of these theories are highly flawed and unsupported by any kind of scientific research. Gardner's multiple intelligences is simply a theory that can't be proved scientifically, while the idea that specific parts of our brain alone conduct certain functions is patently false.

- A true polymath is someone who possesses three components of knowledge: breadth, depth, and integration. This is also known as cross-pollination. Such a person has acquired expertise in at least a few different domains, and can successfully integrate those domains together instead of treating them as unrelated and distinct subjects or skills. So a scientist who is also artistically inclined can use the latter to aid his research in ways that will make him more successful than the average member of his field.

Chapter 2. How to Increase Learning and Skill Transfer

As we've discussed before, perhaps the trickiest part of becoming a polymath is integrating all your knowledge from disparate disciplines toward one common task. The contents of this chapter are aimed at making this step of achieving polymathy simpler than it appears.

The main way we'll do this is through a concept called transfer of learning. Such a transference takes place every time you use something you've learned in a particular context for a different context. In a way, we're constantly using this technique to learn new things without realizing it. We always acquire new knowledge and skills using what we already know.

A simple example of this is when you try to learn math by relating concepts based on their relevance to your business or finances. Similarly, you might learn how to calculate percentages in a math class, and if you're able to use the same concept to calculate your tip at a restaurant, you've successfully transferred your learning from one domain to another.

Unfortunately, learning transfers don't always occur the way we need them to. We often fail to understand how our knowledge from one context can apply to another, and even end up making the wrong connections. However, once you understand the mechanisms and techniques underlying this process, you'll be able to easily exploit the way we naturally learn to acquire knowledge and skills efficiently.

The theory on transfer of learning was developed by researchers Edward Thorndike and Robert Woodworth back in 1901. At the time, the dominant paradigm for learning was something called the doctrine of formal discipline. This is fairly similar to the biological view we discussed before in that proponents of this theory hold that the brain is divided into specific faculties like attention, memory, logic, language, and so on.

To improve performance on a particular task, it was thought that a person needed to improve the faculty that their task relied on. So if someone wanted to strengthen their argumentation skills, they needed to become better at logic by practicing math. Similarly, becoming a more capable writer depended on linguistic skills, which could be refined by learning difficult languages like Latin.

Though this theory supposedly traces its origins to Plato in Ancient Greece, it has now been debunked largely as a result of Thorndike and Woodworth's research. They didn't believe that general skills like logic could affect all tasks that were meaningfully related to those skills. However, what they did acknowledge was that transfer of learning required some degree of overlap between the domains through which knowledge or skills were being transferred.

This interpretation of the transfer of learning model is called the identical components theory. Though there are as many as six different theories on how exactly learning transfers take this place, the identical components theory remains the most influential of the lot.

According to this theory, transfers of learning cannot take place if the domain to which learning is being transferred has nothing in common with the original one. For example, knowing how to sew probably won't help you become a faster runner. As such, while the disciplines and skills you learn to become a polymath need to be sufficiently different from each other to result in creative breakthroughs, they cannot be completely unrelated. It is also the case that the greater the resemblance between the two domains, the easier it is to transfer your knowledge.

Another crucial element of learning transfers is the concept of an active learner. Traditionally we think of learning as a one-way process. A teacher, author, or course instructor simply gives us information, steps to follow, tips and tricks to absorb and utilize. While this method is perfectly suitable for acquiring new knowledge, it isn't the best way to learn and use what you've acquired.

For that, and to facilitate transfer of learning, we must bring our individual and social experiences to the table as well, using our pre-existing knowledge while revising, reorganizing, and reinterpreting it. The method of learning must be tailored to your needs, and elements like your approach, your mental state, confidence or anxiety levels, all play a role in how transferable your learning will eventually be.

Being an active learner means being aware of all of these factors and modifying your learning routines accordingly. If you hate doing math but force yourself to push through it, you're unlikely to be able to think creatively when the time comes to apply your math skills in the real world. However, if you're passionate about reading, you're more likely to be able to use what you've read in a debate or discussion.

Thus, we must aim to be active, enthusiastic learners wherever possible. Some ways to do this are to constantly try and relate your learning materials with your lived experience. If you play sports, you can use math to calculate different statistics based on which sport you play. Similarly, if you're a businessman trying to learn law, you can utilize your knowledge of various topics within law through their relevance to your business in matters such as employee contracts, permissions, ethics, and so on.

Another tactic you can use to become an active learner is to develop curiosity for your subject. This ties into the point about relating learning to your life as well. Try to find new and innovative ways in which your topics might be relevant to other aspects of your life. Ask yourself in what ways you can use the knowledge you're acquiring to your benefit, how you can ensure the skills you're learning will lead to self-improvement in the long-term, etc.

Not only will this approach improve the rate at which you can transfer your learning, but it will also help you choose and add disciplines and skills to your repertoire and enhance your polymathic abilities.

To further our knowledge of learning transfers and implement it productively in our education, we need to familiarize ourselves with the various types of transfers that have been theorized. While they are important in their own right, these types will also be central to understanding the various stages of a learning transfer as they normally occur. Different theorists classify learning tasks in various ways, but we'll divide them broadly into two camps.

The first camp includes positive and negative transfers. As the names suggest, positive transfers are those where previously acquired knowledge successfully result in improvements when learning something else. So if you learn how to count and use that to master addition, that's a positive transfer. A negative transfer is simply the reverse, wherein knowledge acquired in one domain actively hinders learning in another context.

An example of this is trying to learn how to drive right-sided vehicles when one has previously driven only left-sided vehicles. It's very likely that you'll find the former much easier if you'd simply learned to drive right-sided vehicles first than after becoming familiar with the latter. (Leberman et al, 2006)

The second camp of transfers includes several types that can be subdivided into binary categories. The first such category is simple vs. complex transfers. Simple transfers occur when acquired knowledge can easily be transferred to another context. A simple example of this is learning how to launch an application or laptop. Once you learn how to launch a particular application, you've learned how to start all of them as a result of simple transfer. On the other hand, complex transfers require good judgement to transpose something learned in one context to another.

To illustrate this, let's assume you've grown up learning the imperial system of measurements. You're traveling from the US to Canada and encounter metric units like kilometers. If you're able to use those numbers to convert from imperial to metric and calculate how much distance you've covered, you've successfully used a complex transfer to get the right answer. (Leberman et al, 2006)

The next binary is automatic and mindful transfers. Automatic transfers occur subconsciously, without the need for any active interference in the learning transfer. If you engage in academic writing and publishing, this will automatically improve your writing skills in other contexts as well. You don't need to consciously employ the refinements you've acquired over the course of your academic work.

Conversely, mindful transfers occur when you consciously use knowledge from one area in another. Mindful transfers take place between less closely related subjects, such as using mathematical concepts when creating visual art. Both simple and complex transfers are types of mindful transfers, since they require your active judgement for successful execution. (Leberman et al, 2006)

The last type of binary consists of specific and non-specific transfers. Specific transfers involve situations wherein the learner can clearly identify similarities between knowledge they have already acquired and the new context where they are seeking to apply it.

For example, if you use arguments based on deductive logic for philosophical writings, you can use those same arguments to establish claims in other social science disciplines. The subject changes, but deductive argumentation can be applied in both cases. (Royer 1979)

Non-specific transfers are those where there aren't any clearly observable similarities between your past and current learning. So say you've worked with animals and learned how to build trust with them. If you use your learning with animals to also build trust with humans, you've completed a non-specific transfer because it isn't obvious that trust techniques that work with animals would also work with humans.

Non-specific transfers are the key to developing polymathy. Most people can engage in simple or specific transfers, but the ability to transfer learning between fields and contexts that don't have any obvious connection is key to the polymath's potential for boundless success. (Royer 1979)

The Six Stages of Learning Transfers

Now that we know which types of learning transfers exist, we can use these concepts to refine the way we learn and acquire knowledge in the most efficient manner possible. To aid us in this endeavor, we'll use Robert Haskell's taxonomy of learning transfers.

This is basically the six stages in which learning transfers take place. Depending on which stages you reach with particular subjects or skills, you can employ different types of learning transfers to hone your polymathic abilities. These six stages are described below:

Level 1: Non-specific transfer

This stage of learning transfer is called non-specific because everything we learn is acquired as a result of what we've learned in the past. For example, we can't learn calculus if we don't know anything about math. We first need to understand numbers, use numbers to learn addition and similar operations, then build on that knowledge to learn algebra, trigonometry, geometry, and finally, calculus. Most of our ordinary processes of learning proceed in a similar manner: we learn new things based on what we already know.

Level 2: Application Transfer

This stage of the learning transfer process involves practically applying the knowledge we've acquired in the first step. So if we've just learned basic addition and subtraction, we can use that to track our daily expenditures.

Level two generally involves the use of specific transfers because we're still only superficially familiar with the subject we've learned, and require practice and application to solidify our new . For this and the previous level, the main task at hand is learning effectively. Once you manage that, you'll be ready to transfer your knowledge from the next stage onwards.

Level 3: Context Transfer

Context transfer involves the use of your knowledge for a situation that is slightly different from the one in which you initially acquired it. This is the stage where you're most susceptible to negative transfers, since it is fairly easy to transpose your knowledge in wrong ways through false assumptions.

For example, if you're accustomed to writing in more academic and formal language, you might be tempted to use the same approach for more informal writing. However, non-academic writing requires linguistic skills that are somewhat different, and persisting with formal language in such contexts can be an example of a negative transfer. On the other hand, if you can successfully simplify your language to make it more accessible, you'll be ready to proceed to the next stage.

Level 4: Near Transfer

This stage of the learning process is an extension of the previous one. Here you continue to apply your acquired knowledge in situations that are similar to the one where you were originally exposed to it.

So if you were to learn how to drive a car with manual transmission and use that knowledge to drive a truck with manual transmission, you've completed a near transfer. Becoming adept at this will be key to transferring your knowledge in more sophisticated ways, since this step ensures that your transferences are positive.

Level 5: Far Transfer

This is where you start getting close to developing polymathy as a result of learning transfers. Far transfers test your ability to take a piece of learning or knowledge and apply it in some context that is entirely dissimilar to the one where you acquired it. Say that while learning math you've realized it's a good strategy to be careful with your steps and consider alternative answers to the question.

If you apply this same strategy while making investments, you've completed a far transfer. Once you're able to master far transfers, you'll have a much easier time achieving polymathy because this step necessarily demands that you integrate what you've learned in ways that are new and innovative.

Level 6: Displacement/Creative Transfer

The final stage of learning transfers takes the integrative skills we acquired in the previous step to the next level. Being successful at creatively transferring your knowledge is the pinnacle of polymathic abilities, and is sure to lead to new discoveries, inventions, and skills that are pathbreaking in their own right.

An example of creative transfer is this. Say you jump in the air and feel yourself being pulled down due to gravitational force. Later, you enter an elevator and feel yourself accelerated upwards at a similar rate as the one that pulled you down while jumping. If you can connect the dots, the upward acceleration from the lift and the downward pull of gravity are actually the same thing. Einstein was the first to discover this phenomenon, and he called it the Principle of Equivalence.

It is transfers of this nature that qualify as displacement. The ability of Einstein and others like him to regularly transfer their knowledge in this manner is the central reason why they have been so successful in their fields. By working your way up the six steps listed here, you could similarly develop abilities that every polymath needs in their arsenal.

The Science Behind Learning Transfer

Now that you know the types of transfers that exist and the various stages of learning transfers, we'll discuss some scientifically backed techniques that you can utilize to enhance the efficiency of both your learning and your ability to transfer it to other domains. Here they are:

1) Those who develop skills while learning will be more successful at transference

This first tip essentially states that practically applying what you've learned is better than simply learning it. For example, say your job involves learning how to operate a certain power tool. You could learn how to use this tool through a more hands-on approach and actually use it, or you could simply read about how to use it and learn that way.

According to research, the former method will be more productive at enabling you to transfer your learning. To implement this tip more generally, try to create as many practical applications from your learning as is possible. If you're learning math, use it to calculate things in your everyday life. If you're studying political science, relate it to the news you consume. (Thalheimer 2020: 6)

2) Individuals who learn concepts while studying will be better at transfer

This point is closely related to the former one. Assuming your learning doesn't involve the acquiring of skills, what you need to do is form concepts that can then be transferred to other contexts. Of course, if you have neither concepts nor skills, then there won't be anything to transfer. One easy way to form concepts from your studies is to create abstractions out of them so that they are more generally applicable.

So if you've learned that being careful and cross-checking alternative answers is useful through math, you can use that as a general rule in writing, investments, etc.

3) Learners who are enthusiastic about applying their knowledge to their work are more likely to be successful

This tip goes back to our concept of the active learner, wherein your experiences and emotional states as an individual are key to your learning abilities. If you're motivated and enthusiastic about the thing you're learning, you're going to find it much easier to be creative with what you know. On the other hand, if you dislike, say, physics, you'll probably minimize the ways in which you use it.

However, if you're able to cultivate curiosity and interest in the subject, you're much more likely to integrate and apply it practically to your daily life, as well as with other subjects you learn. (Thalheimer 2020: 6)

4) Learners who are provided with early opportunities to practically apply their knowledge through work are more successful at transference

This is another slightly obvious tip given how we're prone to forgetting things soon after we learn them. Motivations to remember and practice can also fade over time, and distractions multiply simultaneously. Hence, you might well find yourself having learned something interesting or useful only to forget it due to the lack of practical application.

By finding relevant uses for your knowledge, you ensure that what you've learned stays with you longer. Doing this in the correct ways also results in positive transfers, which eventually allow you to engage in more complex forms of transfer.

5) Focus on near transfers more than far transfers, at least initially

Far transfers, as ingenious as they are when done correctly, are rare and can often result in negative transfers. Near transfers are much more reliable because we're normally only good at taking knowledge we've acquired and transferring it to some context we've already experienced or practiced. So if you've been learning math, use it to calculate tips at restaurants, the return on your investments, etc. If you try to upend established physics-based principles based on math, you'll likely fail.

Having said that, far transfers are not entirely beyond reach and can be essential to polymathic abilities. Once you have near transfers practiced and perfected, there is no harm in trying to apply your skills in more diverse and creative ways. If you're successful, this can only lead to something ground-breaking.

6) The Self-Efficacy Hypothesis

This hypothesis states that if you feel more able to succeed in applying your knowledge in your work or in practical matters, you will actually be more likely to succeed as well. It's a self-fulfilling prophecy. However, this still leaves the question of how one can believe themselves more able to succeed.

The answer to this quandary is two-fold. The first component is confidence or optimism based on competence, while the second is initiating learning application. Some caution is warranted when it comes to belief in your own ability, since in some cases this has been shown to have a negative effect on transference. Too much can be harmful, but a cautious optimism will likely be helpful in your pursuits.

7) The Role of a Learner's Perceptions

While we've covered elements such as perceptions of self-efficacy and enthusiasm as playing a role in effectively transferring knowledge, there are several other important learner perceptions to consider as well. These include a person's perception of support, positive feedback and outcomes when they apply their learning, of their topics as generally relevant, perceiving themselves to be ready, expectations of job improvement and better performance, etc.

As the list suggests, much of this has to do with the way others perceive you applying your knowledge. If you think your knowledge application will be poorly received, won't be appreciated, or won't have any meaningful impact on your life, you're less likely to successfully transfer your learning. However, if you're able to improve your perceptions of these factors by staying optimistic, your chances of success increase drastically.

Guidelines for Successful Transfer of Learning

This section on learning transfer takes everything we've learned throughout this chapter and combines it to form one definitive set of guidelines that will help you master learning transfers throughout your quest to achieve polymathy. No matter which stage you're at with respect to your studies and application of knowledge, these guidelines will boost your efficiency in profound ways, enabling you to absorb more, forget less, and apply the maximum knowledge possible.

1) Metacognition

This first guideline is one of the most important in this entire list, and will significantly improve your learning transfer more than most other tips and tricks you'll come across.

Metacognition is the process of thinking about your thinking, and using this deeper level of thought to regulate your cognition and manage your behavior to make achieving goals easier. People who are good at metacognition can easily evaluate the pattern of their reasoning and redirect in more productive ways. This is primarily done through your inner voice, or the self-talk that most of us experience.

If you've ever experienced yourself spiraling into a negative thought pattern because of the way you talk to yourself, you're likely aware of the costs of a negative inner voice. The thought of wanting to learn complex subjects might immediately bring forth doubt and apprehension at your abilities to be able to do so effectively.

Metacognition helps you make your self-talk more positive, and it does this by encouraging you to ask yourself a lot of questions. In this case, you might recognize that you have no real reason to worry about outcomes until you actually attempt to learn those subjects, and that you're as likely to be successful as anyone else. Practice this skill of metacognition by asking yourself questions while studying similar to the ones listed below:

- *Does this subject connect well to another domain of knowledge that is related or unrelated?* If you're reading about ethics, think about how that might play a role in your business.

- *Where else have I come across this idea?* If you're studying economics and see that most models assume humans to be a rational, utility-maximizing entity, you might realize that you've come across this notion of humans being rational entities in the history of Enlightenment.

- *How difficult was it for me to grasp this?* Say you struggled to understand how voting behavior works in a democracy. If that's the case, you'll likely have difficulty transferring your learning here to other domains. As such, keep asking yourself this question, and if the answer is "more than normal," spend more time studying the concept.

- *Can I break this down into smaller parts?* Say a person wants to learn graphic design. Instead of trying to learn all they can about this one big topic, they can instead break it down into smaller parts and learn about them individually to better understand graphic design as a whole.

- *How would I explain this to a child?* This is an excellent way to gauge how well you know something. Imagine yourself trying to explain what you've learned to a five-year-old and see how well you do. If you succeed, you've grasped your content well.

- *Why is this important to know?* This question will help you connect your content with other similar topics. You might be studying law to get a better idea of the norms and rules that govern your society, or biology to know how our bodies work. Use such reasons to connect these to other disciplines.

- *What questions does this raise for me?* If you get into the habit of constantly questioning what you're learning, it'll help you see how your knowledge is connected to other things in the world. So after studying Freudian theory you might wonder why it doesn't discuss women much, or what basis is there for his structural model, etc.

- *What, if anything, surprises me about this?* This question is a good way to develop curiosity for the content you're studying. For example, if you're learning theology, you might be surprised by any number of lines in the religious texts you encounter. Dispel those doubts through additional research, and try to connect the answers you find with other, unrelated domains of knowledge.

2) Engage yourself in similar contexts

This guideline demands that you expose yourself to situations where you can successfully complete near transfers. Take the thing you're studying and apply it to the real world in any number of ways that you can come up with. So if you're studying ethics, use your knowledge to question whether you should donate to a beggar you come across.

Similarly, if you're learning how to use Excel, there's probably a way in which that will come in handy for your job. You can use it to store extensive datasets, solve complex mathematical equations, present your data using charts and graphs, etc. Find whichever functions of Excel apply to your work or learning and practice using them to solidify the knowledge you've gained.

3) Keep looking for connections

While you're learning anything new, repeatedly ask yourself whether this connects to anything else that you're aware of. Is learning biology going to help you stay healthier? Is knowing chemistry going to aid you in your cooking skills? Will your knowledge of math help you produce music?

The easier you're able to spot connections, the better your chances of being able to transfer your learning. As you train yourself to do this, you'll be able to find more connections quicker than before, which will ultimately help you take a big step toward achieving polymathy.

4) Practice extensively

This is applicable especially when you're trying to acquire certain skills. Use them in practical ways as often as you can. This will give you much-needed practice that will eventually lead to the skill becoming automatic for you. The automation of skills is often necessary to facilitate near transfers, and eventually far as well as creative transfers.

If you're studying something more academic, one way in which you can utilize this guideline is to constantly revisit your subject matter through notes, flash cards, summaries, etc. Similarly, if you want to learn how to play the guitar, practice chords and strumming until they flow automatically through your muscle memory. This will help you retain more details while also strengthening your general recollection of concepts, skills and theory.

5) Practice extensively in varied contexts

For complex and far transfers to become more natural to you, it isn't enough to keep practicing your knowledge in similar contexts. You also need to challenge yourself by taking what you've learned and using your judgement to see how that might relate to more unrelated domains of knowledge.

So if you're learning how to draw, dabble in different art forms rather than sticking to the one you're comfortable with. You can experiment with line drawing, doodling, cartoons, architectural drawings, and others. This will broaden the range of applications you can use your learning for, which in turn helps you retain more of what you've learned.

6) Focus on first principles

To successfully apply your knowledge in various spheres of life, you need to recognize the underlying principles at play.

Academic disciplines can especially seem to be detached from reality and existing in a world of their own, but all that theory is intricately connected to routine life as we know it. The same concept applies when it comes to skills. We generally learn skills to be used for some specific purpose, but if we think about what we're actually doing through that skill, we can discover more uses for the same activity.

Say you play a sport and do a series of warm-up exercises before beginning to play. You might realize that you can use those same exercises to limber up after waking in the morning, because what you're essentially doing is getting rid of stiffness in various parts of your body. Similarly, first principles can be extracted from much of what we learn, and doing this consciously will help you make learning transfers much easier.

7) Vary the ways in which you consume the media you use to learn

If your main source of learning material is books, you might want to incorporate some audio into your learning routine. Alternatively, if you prefer to listen to your books, you might want to add more videos to your studying. According to multimedia learning theory, engaging our visual and verbal channels by dividing material between them prevents our cognitive processes from being overloaded.

This technique allows you to learn more efficiently. If you're learning how to cook, don't just read recipes, look at videos too. Alternatively, if you're learning how to play an instrument, don't just watch tutorials, read about techniques as well. Generally, it's a good idea to utilize books, videos, podcasts, and courses as resources for learning due to the way they present information, and this helps diversify the way you absorb content as well.

8) Utilize Random Practice Schedules

Say you've learned a variety of tasks or skills in a short amount of time while training for a job. Normally our instincts would be to practice them in the order of learning, going from task one to task two, then to task three and so on. However, studies show you'll be much better off if you adopt a more random schedule to practice what you've learned. While the former technique is effective during training, once that's over you should adopt a more dynamic schedule for best results.

Let's say you've learned a series of tasks in your training program that are relevant to your workflow. This could be working tools in a certain order, performing a set of tasks regularly, etc. Instead of doing these in the order you were taught, performing them in a randomized manner will be more conducive to learning, retaining and flexibly utilizing the information you've acquired.

Problem-Based Learning

There is an urban legend about novice metalworkers. Their teachers tell them to carve a complex structure out of a solid block of metal with only hand tools at their disposal. After they complete this tedious and seemingly impossible problem, what do you suppose was accomplished by the student? They became true experts with hand tools.

What about famous Mr. Miyagi from *The Karate Kid* movie? Who can forget how he taught his student, Daniel-san, how to perform hard labor? And yet, after this goal was achieved, it turns out Daniel-san learned the basics of karate.

Through solving a problem or reaching for a goal, learning was made inevitable.

Problem-based learning (PBL) is where you start with a problem that needs to be solved, and you force learning through the process of solving that problem. You try to accomplish a goal that necessitates learning. Instead of setting out to learn X, the idea is to set a goal of solving problem Y, and in the process, learning X. Of course, this is pure learning transfer.

Usually, we learn information and skills in a linear manner. In school, a traditional approach is commonly used: material is given to us, we memorize it, and we are shown how that information solves a problem. This might even be how you structure your learning when you're by yourself—because you don't know anything different.

PBL requires you to identify what you already know about the problem and what knowledge and resources you still need, to figure out how and where to obtain that new information, and finally how to piece together a solution to the problem. This is far different from the linear approach of most schooling. We can draw on my failed romantic escapades as an adolescent for illustration.

I wanted to impress *Jessica from Spanish class*. It's a noble and mighty motivation that has been the impetus for many changes in the life of a young (and old) male. We were in the same Spanish class, and I had the good fortune of sitting directly behind her. It turns out she wasn't too interested in Spanish, so she would constantly turn around and ask me for help.

I would first get caught in her eyes, but then my spirits would fall because I realized I had no idea how to answer her questions. *What if she started asking the other guys in the class? I didn't want that!*

With that in mind, I began to study and learn Spanish so she would have all the more reason to continue turning around and talking to me. It's amazing what you can do when you have the proper motivation for it, and I probably became fluent more quickly than anyone in the class that year. What's more, I would look up obscure or complex phrases solely to impress her, just in case I had the opportunity.

I created a massive set of flashcards. They started with one word on the back of each card, but by the end of the school year, they had three to four sentences on the back of each, all in Spanish. I got an A+ in the class, one of the few in my high school career, but I never did get anywhere with Jessica.

This is a classic case of PBL—I wanted to solve the problem of X (Jessica), but I ended up learning Y (Spanish) in the process.

Of course, the key for us is to be deliberate about the problem you spend your time solving, so what you learn helps you accomplish what you want. It can be as simple as wanting to master a new scale on the guitar, and attempting to play a difficult song that incorporates that scale. You can see how focusing on solving a problem can be more helpful and educational than simply reading a textbook or hearing a lecture. There's certainly something to be said for firsthand experience.

PBL has been around in one form or another since John Dewey's pivotal 1916 book *Democracy and Education: An Introduction to the Philosophy of Education*. One of the basic premises of Dewey's book was learning by doing.

Fast forward to the 1960s, when PBL had its modern start. Medical schools started using real patient cases and examples to train future doctors. Indeed, this is still how many medical students learn to diagnose and treat patients. Rather than memorize an endless supply of facts and figures, medical students went through the diagnostic process and picked up information along the way. That's exercising a different muscle than reading and writing notes.

What questions should they ask of the patient? What information do they need from the patient? What tests should be run? What do the results of those tests mean? How do the results determine the course of treatment? By asking and answering all of these questions in the process of PBL, medical students ultimately learn how to treat patients.

Imagine that a medical student is presented with the following case: A sixty-six-year-old male patient comes in to the office complaining of recent shortness of breath.

What are the next steps in this blank canvas?

In addition to medical, family, and social histories, the student would want to find out how long the symptoms have been occurring, at what time of day, what activities lead to shortness of breath, and whether anything makes it worse or better. The physical exam, then, becomes problem-focused: check blood pressure, listen to heart and lungs, check legs for edema, etc. Next the student would determine whether any lab tests or X-rays need to be done. And then based on those results, the student would come up with a plan for treatment. And that's just for starters.

If the instructor wanted the student to learn about how to deal with potential heart problems, they accomplished that. By applying their investigative skills to real-world cases, the learning was more realistic, more memorable, and more engaging for the medical students. Research has shown that when learning is problem-based for medical students, clinical reasoning and problem-solving skills improve, learning is more in-depth, and concepts are integrated for better overall understanding of the material.

PBL forces students to take ownership of the solution and approach, and they absorb a concept or set of information in an entirely different manner. Instead of simply solving for X, they must come up with the entire equation that leads to X. It involves a deep sense of exploration and analysis, both of which lead to a greater understanding than simple regurgitation.

PBL leads to greater self-motivation as well because rather than learning for learning's sake, there is a real-life issue at stake, with real-life consequences.

Living in the "real world," we typically aren't given case scenarios or assigned to group projects (at least not in the elementary-school sense of the phrase) to assist in our learning goals. Whether we know it or not, we can put ourselves in a position to enhance our learning by directing it to specific purposes. What follows are a few examples of how to find a problem that will necessitate further learning on your part.

Meal Planning. For instance, you want to solve a problem of dealing with delayed and frantic dinners. You choose this task because, besides solving the problem of unnecessary stress and anxiety, you will learn how to become a better cook in every sense of the word. You want to solve X (stressful meals) but along the way also learn Y (how to cook better).

So, what steps would you take to become more proficient in the kitchen? One way would be to implement a meal-planning system to allow you to try new recipes and techniques. First, determine what do you already know about the problem? Your family needs to eat. Recipes would be nice, perhaps starting out easy and then becoming more involved. You need the ingredients to make those recipes, a schedule of what meal to serve when, and a strategy for how you will tackle the more advanced techniques.

What do you still need to know? You need actual recipes and ingredient lists. You need some sort of organized plan for when you'll serve each dinner, probably a calendar. You may want to identify specific skills you want to acquire.

Where will you obtain new information to help solve this problem? Maybe you start by asking members of your family to share their three favorite meals with you. Then you hop on Pinterest to find some recipes. From there, you make a grocery list, maybe on a notepad, or your computer in a Word doc, or a grocery app you find. Next you need to put your meals onto a calendar. Again, you may do this on your computer, or you might find a meal-planning printable or app. And maybe you want to explore online grocery ordering with delivery or pickup to further save time (and probably impulse spending). You'll need to figure out how you will learn new cooking approaches: reading, YouTube videos, going to a class, etc.

By making a strategic plan to enhance your cooking skills, you have solved your mealtime chaos by using PBL! You identified what you already knew (you need ideas about what new skills you wanted to learn, meal ideas, recipes, a grocery list), figured out what you still needed to know (the techniques themselves, specific recipes, ingredient lists, a meal calendar), and where you found that information (family, Pinterest, apps, books, online, computer, etc.).

Not only have you created a plan for your family's upcoming meals, you have devised a strategy to use moving forward week after week, month after month, all the while learning new techniques and improving your cooking skills. By developing a meal-planning strategy, you are saving time and money, and you may see a decrease in chaos and an increase in family satisfaction with meals. Call it killing two birds with one stone.

The Broken Toaster. Let's consider a more complicated problem. Your toaster seems to no longer be working, and you have toast for breakfast every day. You've always wanted to learn more about electronics and put to use what you learned years ago. You want to solve X (broken toaster) but along the way also learn Y (basic electronics skills). What would PBL look like in this somewhat daunting scenario?

The first step is to determine what you already know. Your toaster isn't functioning. You're pretty handy and would consider fixing it yourself. You know a little about wiring. And you really like your toaster, a model that is no longer made.

What, then, do you need to know to solve this problem? You will need to determine the specific cause of your toaster malfunction. You will potentially require some instruction for aspects of the problem outside your current skill set. You will need tools and supplies as well as the time and a place to work on your toaster.

In the information-gathering stage, you will disassemble your toaster to try to determine the problem. You may look online or go to the library for a "fix-it" manual for small appliances. There are YouTube videos you could consult for a visual tutorial. Then, once you've determined the issue, learned how to fix it, and made the repair, you're back in business with your toaster.

Problem-based learning provides a helpful framework for a thoughtful, organized way to approach a problem, challenge, or dilemma in order to learn a new skill or new information. You can think of PBL as a series of steps as demonstrated in the examples above.

1. Define your problem.
2. Determine what you already know.
3. List potential solutions and choose the one most likely to succeed.
4. Break the steps into action items (a timeline often helps).

5. Identify what you still need to know and how you will get that information.

There are some distinct advantages to PBL. Not only will you have better retention of what you have learned, you will generally gain a deeper understanding of the problem and solutions than if you had taken a less focused approach. While it can seem like a problem-based approach has too many steps and will take too long, generally PBL tends to save you time in the long run since you aren't randomly trying less-well-thought-out solution after solution. Planning and formulating a systematic plan ultimately saves you time, and often money, too! That is the benefit of directly solving a problem—you get to the heart of what matters.

PBL can be applied to most any aspect of your life. You may have to get creative in how to design a problem or goal around something you want to learn, but this is the type of learning technique that will skyrocket your progress. After all, there's only so much we can gain without applying what we know to the real world via learning transfer.

Takeaways

- While you're learning to be a polymath, perhaps the most difficult task you'll face is to integrate your knowledge from different disciplines. The concept of *learning transfer* will make this part of achieving polymathy significantly simpler.
- A learning transfer occurs when you use knowledge or skills acquired in a certain context in an area that is different from the original one. There are several types of learning transfers. Among these are positive and negative transfers. The former is simply a successful learning transfer, whereas a negative transfer occurs when knowledge acquired in one context hinders learning in another. Then there are simple and complex transfers. Simple transfers occur when you transfer learning from one context to another one that is similar

to the first, whereas complex transfers involve transference to more disparate contexts. Finally, there are also specific and non-specific transfers. When the context to which you're transferring your knowledge has clear similarities with the original one, a specific transfer occurs. However, when there are no apparent similarities between the two contexts, a non-specific transfer occurs.

- There are several science-backed tips you can follow to improve the chances of a positive transfer. Generally, those who are enthusiastic about their learning and are often to apply it to different settings are more successful at transferring it to other contexts. It has also been shown that people who are optimistic and confident about their ability to transfer their learning are more able to do so.

- In addition to these tips, there are some guidelines you can follow to maximize your ability to transfer your learning. Primary among these is learning the concept of metacognition, which is the process of being able to think about your thinking, and use that to regulate your thought and learning process by asking yourself questions. Besides this, practice transference in different contexts, far and near, use different types of media while learning, and keep looking for connections between what you've learned and unrelated contexts.

- Problem-based learning is where you deliberately choose a problem to solve, or a goal to achieve, which will necessitate the learning of a skill. In essence, instead of setting out to learn X, the idea is to set a goal of solving problem Y, and in the process, learn X. This will keep you engaged and motivated, and also drive deeper learning because you will take ownership of something and put all the pieces together yourself. For instance, you will need to identify what you know, what you don't know, identify solutions, and take action.

Chapter 3. Breaking Knowledge Down

Imagine this scenario: You're an academic scholar and are presenting your research on German idealism at a conference in front of an audience that is only passingly familiar with philosophy and probably not even aware of what idealism is. Considering that the German idealists were some of the most complicated and difficult thinkers in all of philosophy, how would you present your information in a way that is easily accessible to the average person?

This chapter will teach you how to take complex pieces of knowledge and break them down so that anyone can comprehend them easily. The main tool we'll be using for this is analogical thinking. Using analogies effectively in your learning will help you grasp concepts better and minimize the chances of negative transfers as you integrate your knowledge from disparate disciplines. This, in turn, will be key to you achieving polymathy.

An analogy is just a comparison drawn between two seemingly unrelated concepts. In our normal conversations, we use analogies fairly often, sometimes even without realizing it. Remarks like saying someone is as tall as a giraffe, using similes such as "fits like a glove," and generally saying that a particular thing is "like" something else are all examples of analogies.

Academic Analogies

While the above examples are informal, conversational analogies, there are also more academic analogies that can be used to teach ourselves different concepts. Academic analogies derive their effectiveness from the fact that they force you to transfer something you've learned to another context. To do this well, you inevitably need to have some grasp over your subject matter, and this is why analogies are so often used for testing and assessing students on their learning.

Here is an example of how you can use academic analogies in your learning. Let's say you want to craft an analogy for the role that laws play in a constitution. The academic analogy format has four spaces, A, B, C, and D, that are placed in the following manner: ___ (A) : ___ (B) :: ___ (C) : ___ (D). (Heick 2020)

Fill in "law" and "constitution" in the A and B spaces respectively. What you need to do now is fill C with something that plays the role of laws, and D with something that it plays that role for. Laws are the main component of a constitution, so we're looking for an object and the thing that it majorly consists of. One example of this is code in digital applications. So we'd feed that in using the same format—Law : Constitution :: Code: Digital Applications.

It's natural to be unsure of whether your analogy really holds, and grappling with whether your comparison fits well is part of absorbing your original concept in the right manner. Think of ways to justify the comparison. Does law play the same role for constitutions as code does for applications?

The answer is yes. Constitutions are made up of laws, and digital applications rely on coding for everything from design, to features, speed, and more. Without laws or code, both of these entities lose their essential feature. You can't have a constitution without laws, nor are applications without code possible.

Let's consider another example; this time we'll think of an analogy for fish and river. Fishes are found in rivers, so we need to identify something that is commonly found in a certain area. One example could be animals on land, or birds in the sky. We'll note this using the same format—Fish : River :: Animals : Land. While this way of coming up with analogies might initially seem somewhat dry, this activity will become much more fun as you practice it further. Besides, you'll surely notice the learning advantages it gives you.

The examples we've discussed so far are of a particular type of academic analogy. There are fourteen different types in total, and each can be used in different contexts based on the kind of connection you're making between the original two components, and the thing they're being compared to. Each of these also promote creative thinking in their own ways, so use them appropriately.

Synonym

Here you simply have to find a synonym for the thing you're learning. Say you're studying deontological ethics. What's another way to say that without the jargon? Here's the answer. First we'll consider two synonyms on the left side for comparison. For our purpose we'll use "beginner" and "novice." One synonym for this term is simply "rules," and that's what we'll fill into

the D space. Beginner: Novice ::
Deontological ethics : Rules.

Antonym

This is the exact reverse of the previous
type of analogy in that you have to name the
opposite of something you're learning. As
before, we'll use an example on the left, and
this time it'll be "beginner" and "master."
Say we're studying the concept of liberty.
What would be an antonym for that?
Servitude. Thus, we have Beginner: Master
:: Liberty : Servitude

Part/Whole

This is the type of analogy we utilized for
our example with laws and video games.
This type of analogy can help you
contextualize what you are learning and see
where it fits in the larger scheme of things.
For this example, we'll use "stars" and
"galaxy" on the left. If you're studying
atomic theory from chemistry, you can use
this to create an analogy between stars in a
galaxy and atoms with molecules, or

molecules and any object. So we have Stars : Galaxy :: Atoms : Molecules.

Cause/Effect

While using this analogy, keep in mind that it is often easy to reverse the order of cause and effect. What appears to be the effect is often the cause, and vice versa, especially when you're studying phenomena in the social sciences. Use the cause/effect analogy to observe whether you've understood the chain of causation correctly.

For example, the rise of cars led to the decline of horse carriages. Say you're studying the theory of nationalism. This concept originated with the French revolution, but did nationalism cause the Revolution, or did the Revolution result in the rise of nationalism? Frame your analogy depending on what you think is the right answer, and justify it accordingly. Here you might end up with Cars : Horse Carriages :: French Revolution : Nationalism, or you might settle on Cars : Horse Carriages :: Nationalism : French Revolution. Your answer and the reasoning behind it will ensure you understand just how one element led to the next.

Thing/Function

This analogy is useful for reflecting upon the practical utility of the thing you're studying by looking for its functions. Alternatively, you can simply draw analogies between a particular concept, event, etc., and analyze the role it plays in a certain context, which also counts as its function. For example, headphones are used to listen to music. Assume you're studying the life of Martin Luther King. What was his role/function in history? Advocating for civil rights. This gives us Headphones : Music :: MLK : Civil Rights.

Thing/Characteristic

Thing/Characteristic is among the simpler types of analogies on this list, but it can still be useful in taking an account of how much you know about a particular concept or object. To use this analogy effectively, name as many characteristics of the thing you're learning as possible and note all of them down.

For example, cotton is soft. If you're studying atomic theory, one characteristic of atoms is that they're minuscule in size. So we have Cotton : Soft :: Atoms : Small. Other characteristics of an atom include the fact that it's the basic component of all objects, it forms chains with other atoms, etc.

Thing/Context

This analogy is very similar to the Part/Whole type in that both act as effective means to contextualize concepts within a certain framework. For example, we generally speak of electronic devices like phones, televisions, etc., in the context of technology. Similarly, we talk of politicians and policies in the context of elections. This gives us Electronic Devices : Technology :: Politicians : Elections.

Example/Type Of

Example/Type Of analogies can be very useful in using your knowledge for far transfers, because often the thing you're studying can be an example of something that belongs to a "type of" from another context altogether. For example, an iPhone is an example or type of a smartphone. Similarly, deontology is an example of a system of ethics. This gives us iPhone: Smartphone :: Deontology: Ethics.

Category/Sub-Category

This type of analogy is almost identical to the previous one. If we use the same example, an iPhone is a subcategory of smartphones, while deontology is a subcategory of ethics.

Fact/Opinion

Fact/Opinion is another analogy that is especially useful for the social sciences. You'll often come across resources that blend facts with opinion, and it pays to be able to differentiate between them. For example, say you hear someone saying, "It's hot." That's a subjective opinion that may or may not apply to you. However, if someone says its 93 degrees outside, that might be based on actual reading of the current temperature.

Similarly, if someone says that a person is tall, your agreement depends on a lot of factors. However, if someone says that the person is 6' 3", you can objectively judge whether they are tall or not. So we have Hot: 93 degrees :: Tall : 6' 3".

Problem/Solution

This type of analogy lets you analyze and compare the solutions to particular issues with those of other problems. So discrimination can be countered by affection and mutual respect, while illnesses and diseases can be healed with medicines. Problem/Solution analogies will probably require the most detail out of all the ones listed here, and like Thing/Characteristic analogies, you can cite multiple solutions to the same problem.

Tips to Make the Most of Analogies

Aside from using different types of analogies to improve your retention of learning materials, there are some science-backed tips you can employ to further enhance how productive these analogies can be for your studies. These are:

1) Use multiple analogies for the same topic

This one goes without saying, but using different types of analogies in your learning will ensure that you've grasped your content beyond just a superficial understanding. Since analogies force you to make transfers mentally, they challenge your comprehension of key concepts in different ways depending on the type you use. Generally, it's a good idea to use as many as you can that seem relevant to your topic.

For example, let's say you're learning about the theory of liberalism. The first type of analogy you can use is Antonym. If we think of hot and cold as opposites, what would be a similar antonym for liberalism? This could be either communism or conservatism. Next, we can utilize Example/Type Of analogies. Liberalism is a type of political ideology, in the same way that iPhones are a type of smartphone.

A third type of analogy we can attempt is Thing/Characteristic. What is a characteristic of liberalism similar to auditory volume as a characteristic of speakers? One answer is human rights. Likewise, you can utilize multiple analogies for your own concepts and topics.

2) Use examples to reaffirm your learning constantly

This insight has been derived from the studies of Daniel Schwartz and John Bransford. The usage of examples is important because it helps novices and beginners learn through their own knowledge of the content of those examples. Experts can skip examples because they are already intimately aware of the subject matter. But in most instances, examples help you make sense of complex ideas and provide yourself with tools to remember them more efficiently.

If you're studying ethical systems, make a note of different situations in which they apply. Should you lie to your friend when you don't want to talk to them by saying you're busy? Why or why not? If you have to divide a pie between three people, what would be the most fair way to cut it? Examples like these liven up your studying, as they make dry content much more realistic and relevant to the world around you.

3) Remember the purpose of the analogy

Oftentimes it is easy to use analogies for understanding particular concepts mechanically, yet forget why the analogy is appropriate in the first place. For example, if a student is asked what mitochondria is, they say "it is the powerhouse of the cell" since that is a standard analogy across biology textbooks. However, many remember the comparison without understanding or having forgotten what it means for mitochondria to be the powerhouse of a cell.

One way to avoid this issue is to frame your analogies in ways that clearly indicate the purpose or role of the comparison. In the case of mitochondria, consider what function it would have to fulfill to be a "powerhouse" for the cell. It would have to provide the cell with power, which is more accurately referred to as energy.

Another thing you can do is to list a few drawbacks of the analogy. "Powerhouse" can imply that it merely stores energy, but in fact mitochondria is responsible for the extracting, processing, and releasing of energy to cells. It isn't enough to simply remember the analogy; you must know why it is an appropriate one to use as well, and these are a few ways to do just that.

4) Reserve analogies for more difficult concepts

While it may be tempting to use analogies throughout your studies, it is advisable to reserve their usage for more complex ideas. Students often find that utilizing analogies for easier concepts and information can cause confusion and clutter.

When something is easily understandable, you don't need to break it down further for better retention. Focus your energy on more difficult concepts, especially since you'll be using multiple analogies for the same concept.

Make a list of all the ones you use, list some drawbacks for each, and use visual cues if possible. Using both visual and text-based cues is a good way to improve retention and understanding according to multimedia learning theory. Also use appropriate comparisons for your analogy on the left-hand side of the academic analogy format. This will make the relation between the main components of your analogy clearer without requiring too much re-reading.

Analogy Thinking

Let's dive a bit deeper into a specific type of analogy thinking.

How might you explain a new business to someone who is clueless in the space? "It's like the Uber of X, except A, B, and C."

When we seek to make ourselves understand, we often default to analogies. They provide instant understanding and context, because our thoughts are able to focus on a singular concept and then slowly start to differentiate to the point of comprehension.

And of course, linking new concepts and information through analogy is another great method to cement learning into the knowledge pool. Despite our natural tendencies, analogies are underrated and overlooked as important parts of human cognition. In contrast to this presumption, some neuroscientists, such as Indiana University Professor Douglas Hofstadter, assert that analogies are the foundation of all human thought.

His reasoning is that analogies allow us to understand categories, and categories are how we discern information and concepts from each other. It's our ability to discern likenesses—a form of analogy-making— that allows us to discern similarities and thus categorize objects in different ways.

This is easy to see if you consider how we categorize animals. To an untrained eye, a dog and a cat might seem distinctly similar. They both have fur, four legs, and a tail, but their different faces, diets, behavior, and evolutionary heritage allow us to differentiate between the two of them. They are comparable animals, analogous to each other, but they are more closely analogous to their own species, and that is what allows us to place them in their respective categories of dog or cat. But all that means is that we would never use dogs to describe cats, or vice versa.

Even more complex, higher-order ideas are formed by making analogies. Consider the more abstract group of mammal. This group compares dogs to cats while counting them as similar, but also includes animals as diverse as the platypus, dolphin, and opossum. No one would look at a dolphin and believe it was similar to a housecat, but the science is very clear. Lactating, having hair or fur, and being warm-blooded are the only criteria that must be met to put creatures into the group of mammal. If they share those characteristics, they are mammals.

Grouping those criteria together allows us to form the higher-order idea of mammal, which enables us to discern which creatures fit the bill. This group of criteria that we simplify into the word *mammal* is what allows us to see dolphins and platypuses as analogous to each other.

Our understanding, and thus the analogies we use to describe the world, evolve as we age and are exposed to ideas in our lives and our cultures. But no matter what we learn, it must be filtered through a brain that categorizes, and thus understands, the world by forming analogies and discerning differences between objects and ideas. When we consciously distinguish different elements and create analogies while learning new information, we speed up the process of integrating our new knowledge into our minds.

Now that we've covered the overall cognitive role and importance of analogy, how can we use it to self-learn and understand more effectively? As we mentioned, analogies provide instant context—a mental model for the information you are looking at—and then you are left to slowly differentiate and flesh out the details.

For instance, earlier we mentioned that new businesses are frequently described as "the Uber of X." Uber is a rideshare company that functions by calling non-taxi drivers to help transport you using their own personal cars. Thus, anything described as "the Uber of X" would be implied to involve people with their own cars, delivering or driving people or things. Okay, we've got a mental image now—a good idea of what's involved, what the purpose is, and how it functions.

Now the important bit of learning comes—how do you differentiate this new business from Uber itself? What nuanced factors make it simply not a clone of Uber? Well, this element, as well as what you are comparing the new business to, is up to you to articulate. When you take a new piece of information and intentionally find a way to create an analogy with it, you are (1) finding a similar model of information that requires understanding enough to compare and contrast two concepts, and (2) further understanding the two models well enough to state how they differ. That's where the deeper learning synthesis occurs.

For instance, what if you wanted to create an analogy around learning the steps involved in creating a new piece of legislation? Abide by the two steps above. You would first find an existing, familiar piece of information that the process for new legislation reminds you of. Search your memory banks for something similar; this type of analysis of major and minor factors is helpful to your learning.

Next, how do they differ? This is where you can clearly demonstrate the difference between concepts, based on a deep understanding. Pick out small details and note how they appear similar but come from totally different motivations. Document what this all means for new legislation.

This is far more than a thought exercise of comparing two different concepts—it's combining old information with new and forcing them to interact toward greater comprehension and memorization.

Using Concrete Examples

Another essential technique for breaking knowledge down is creating concrete examples to deal with abstract concepts. This is useful because abstract ideas often feel vague and are consequently hard to grasp. Human minds are wired to remember specific, concrete things we see and hear, not abstract notions about theories we contemplate. Finding concrete examples that demonstrate abstract concepts is one of the best tools available to bring abstract notions down to Earth and make them easier to understand and remember.

As a quick example, suppose you are learning about the law of supply and demand. You will probably have some concrete examples in your textbook or lecture, but what about imposing one from your own life? Remember that time when you were trying to book a hotel in a city during peak tourism season? The prices were astronomical, and you almost had a hernia when you paid. That's because there was a huge demand, and thus, the supply was shrinking. These factors caused prices to rise, because the market demand supported higher prices where there was short supply.

Take concepts you've learned and complete this process by yourself. You may not be able to come up with concrete examples for everything you're learning, and in that case, you can use hypotheticals to literally construct examples that exemplify the point. Examples force application, and the funny thing about learning is that you'll never know what you don't know until you try to use it.

Like learning how to kick a soccer ball or drive a vehicle, we just have to find out for ourselves, and no amount of reading will ever replace firsthand experience. A concrete example is often the closest we will be able to get to much of the information and concepts we learn. Make it personal to you and you will never forget it.

Similar to analogies, the understanding required to actually construct an intelligible and illustrative example is deep. Simply going through this process will make you see the gaps in your knowledge, and also force you to revisit your entire understanding.

Suppose you are puzzled about the theory of gravity. Create an example of just how quickly you would fall to the ground if you jumped out of the second story, third story, and fourth story of a building. Visualize the concrete feeling of your stomach rushing to your throat, and you can grasp just how powerful the rate of gravity (9.8 meters per second) is. The theory of gravity is almost always described as Isaac Newton's imagining of an apple falling on his head as a very real illustration of how gravity impacts everything on earth.

Whatever the concept, especially ones you are struggling with, strive to create your own concrete example.

For example, the mental state of *courage* is defined as "the ability to do something that frightens one." This is fairly abstract. How might we understand this better?

An obvious example would be a soldier knowingly risking his life by going to war, but fighting bravely regardless. A more accessible example would be the anxiety we feel before and during a job interview or first date, an unease we all try to swallow and push through to take advantage of new opportunities. This example is particularly useful, as it relates an abstract concept to a near-universal human experience the learner can remember and relate to. The more concrete it is to us, the more we feel its impact and ultimately understand it.

Even though not all examples are perfect, they add depth and meaning to our understanding while solidifying abstract concepts into ideas we can easily grasp and remember.

Mind-Mapping

Finally, in your attempts to achieve polymathy, you're bound to be overwhelmed by all the information you come across in your studies. Mind mapping is an invaluable technique that will help you organize the concepts, descriptions, and connections you discover between various topics in a manner that is both simple and easy to remember.

Mind maps will also help you give direction to your study since it makes it easier to know what you've covered already, how it all connects to each other, and which areas you need to know more about.

While there are several ways of illustrating your thoughts and work such as concept webs, spider diagrams, and others, mind mapping has several unique benefits to offer. It allows you to see the bigger picture because of the way mind maps are constructed, thus letting you stay focused on the important parts without getting sidetracked.

The colorful nature of mind maps also helps you retain more of the information you put down in them. Lastly, when studying complex topics, you can use several mind maps to efficiently break down and summarize different subtopics while keeping your material brief and uncluttered.

How to Make a Mind Map

Tony Buzan, the creator of mind maps, has some guidelines on how to effectively make mind maps. All you need for this exercise are some sheets of paper and at least three different colored pens or pencils.

Step 1

Start by placing the sheet of paper horizontally in front of you, zeroing in on the center of the page. You can either use an image related to your main topic or draw a circle and write it within that. Generally, it is a good idea to use symbols, images, and drawings to represent information to facilitate better retention. However, words and bubbles will also do just fine.

Step 2

Draw thick branches that stick out of your central image or bubble in different directions. These can be called your main branches. Use your colored pens to create some contrast, and draw additional bubbles at the end of these branches. Write or draw major subtopics within these bubbles. For example, if you're studying philosophy, your branches can be about different subfields within philosophy, such as ethics, metaphysics, political philosophy, epistemology, etc.

Step 3

Continue making branches within your subtopics and ensure that they are spaced out enough to minimize clutter. So if your subtopic is ethics, you can go further and note schools of thought such as utilitarianism and deontology. For political philosophy, you can have democracy, oligarchy, aristocracy, and tyranny as sub-fields.

Step 4

Keep drawing new branches that further specify the content of the bubbles they extend from. For example, for utilitarianism you can simply write "the greatest happiness of the greatest number," whereas deontology can be a "rules-based theory."

That's all you need to do. It's really this simple. Draw a circle in the center and keep making branches with more bubbles, which in turn have their own branches and bubbles, till you've filled up the entire sheet of paper. When tackling entire disciplines like philosophy or psychology, it might be helpful to make multiple mind maps. This would work exactly the same way, except the middle bubble would contain your sub-topic, such as political philosophy, instead of your larger area of interest. This will help you be more comprehensive in accumulating and organizing everything you've learned.

Here is another example of how you can make a mind map.

Step 1

Say you want to make a mind map about different political ideologies. You can write "political ideologies" in the central bubble and draw four branches from it

Step 2

These branches end with their own bubbles, within which you can write liberalism, communism, anarchism, and fascism. Alternatively, you can use symbols to denote them. Use the Statue of Liberty for liberalism, the face of Karl Marx for communism, Mussolini for fascism, and the symbol of anarchism which is a capital A with a circle around the middle.

Step 3

Within these, draw more branches and bubbles that extend from each of these subtopics. Fill in the relevant information through words or images. So liberalism can have the phrase "liberty, equality, fraternity" in one bubble, private property in another, free and fair elections in the third one, so on and so forth. Similarly, communism can have "state control over the economy," "classless society," "abolition of religion," etc.

Step 4

Continue the above process until you reach the ends of your sheet of paper.

Let's consider one final example of how to create a mind map for your studies.

Step 1

Assume you want to draw a mind map to study US history. Write "US History" in a bubble around the middle of your paper and extend at least six branches from it. You can choose to use more depending on how extensively you're studying the topic, but for our purpose six will suffice.

Step 2

At the end of these main branches, you can note down the major periods or landmark events. So you can start with the arrival of the Pilgrims at Plymouth Rock, proceeding to the American Revolution, and then the Civil War, US involvement in the World Wars, followed by the Cold War, and then lump the rest into post-1990 history.

Step 3

As before, extend branches from these subtopics within US history. For the first part, you may want to cover Thanksgiving, the Pilgrims' interaction with Native Americans, etc. Carry on with major events from the Revolution like the Boston Tea Party, its various causes, the adoption of democracy as a form of rule, and so on. Similarly proceed with the Civil War, World Wars, and Cold War along with their landmark events, notable incidents, outcomes, and statistics.

Step 4

Continue adding more depth to your points and include sufficient detail so you can come back to the map and still glean most of the relevant information pertaining to this topic.

Tips and Tricks to Improve Your Mind Maps

The most basic mind map can be made using just a pen or pencil and with bubbles and branches on paper. However, such a map is unlikely to be memorable, which is one of the key reasons for using mind mapping as a technique in the first place. There are several things you can do to enhance your mind maps and maximize how useful they are in your efforts toward becoming a polymath. The following tips and tricks will help you in that endeavor:

1. Minimize the number of words you use. Keep the information inside your bubbles brief and to the point.
2. Maximize visual aids like colors, symbols, drawings, etc. You can also use written words in different ways. So one main branch from your central bubble can have text written only in lowercase, while another has text that is exclusively uppercase.
3. Emphasize certain words or parts of the text you've included in your map to exhibit their importance.
4. Make the main branches thicker, and gradually reduce the thickness as you proceed deeper into the mind map. This is another visual cue that will help you remember the hierarchy of your information.

5. Don't restrict yourself to bubbles; use different shapes at the end of your main branches and for that entire part of your mind map. These shapes can help you differentiate the various parts of your map and recall them more clearly.

Takeaways

- When you encounter new information from sources that you're unfamiliar with, some of it will undoubtedly be complex and inaccessible. This can often serve as an incentive for people to abandon their quest for polymathy. However, analogies are an extremely powerful tool that makes breaking down complicated information easy and efficient.
- Analogies are essentially comparisons between two seemingly unrelated concepts or skills. To maximize your learning, you'll need to learn how to use what you already know and draw connections to what

you're learning in innovative ways. This forces you to transfer your learning, ensuring you retain more information in the long-term.

- To start using analogies for learning, you'll need to familiarize yourself with academic analogies. These consists of four parts divided into two groups. On the left side, you make a certain type of connection between things you know about, like code in video games. Code is the main building block upon which video games are built. If you're learning law, you'll know that law is to constitution what code is to video games. To use the standard analogy format, we'd state this as: "code : video games :: law : constitution."

- The kind of connection you make on the left side of your analogy varies drastically depending on the type of analogy you use. The two can be synonyms, antonyms, have a part-whole relationship, etc. While learning, you'll need to decide which types fit your topic best, and use as many of them as possible.

- Once you're comfortable with drawing analogies, you can also follow some simple steps to make sure you get the most out of them. Try to refrain from using analogies for simple concepts and reserve them only for difficult ones to avoid confusion. Use plenty of concrete examples to simplify abstract concepts and information. Additionally, you should review the purpose of your analogy from time to time, since it can be easy to remember the comparison but difficult to recall what made it an accurate one.

- One technique that compliments analogies exquisitely is mind mapping. This tool draws connections between different concepts within the same topic to keep track of how they all connect to each other. The most basic way to create a mind map is to start with a circle in the middle of some paper and draw branches that extend from it. Fill these branch-endings with sub-topics and extend even more branches to exhaust the sub-topic. You can use this method to keep track of all your analogies, while also adding additional information relevant to them.

Chapter 4. The Polymathic Mind

Given what we know now about polymaths, the natural question is to ask what we can learn from their approach, and how best we can set ourselves up to succeed in a quickly changing world. This requires of us a little more creative thinking than merely asking, "What skills are valuable in the marketplace right now? What's the next big thing?"

The truth is that successful polymaths are primarily driven by insatiable curiosity, a love for their fields, a yearning for mastery, creativity and expression—or a blend of all of these. They may not share anything in common as far as their fields of expertise go, but they certainly share the same zest for life and set of traits that keep them pushing for more.

Thus it is not enough to simply mimic the end results of polymaths' process. We need to ask *how* they've thought and worked, rather than getting bogged down in the details of *what* they've done. It's about what has spurred them to develop a pi or comb shape instead of remaining as a simple T-shape.

Many people falsely believe that, to remain competitive, they need to upskill in all the fashionable and trending ways. People ask how they can learn to write computer code or trade cryptocurrencies, for example, not because this is where their passion genuinely takes them, but because they're swayed by the stories of tech entrepreneurs who have already gone this (now well-travelled) path.

Unfortunately, this is a losing strategy for two reasons: one because by the time a trend is identifiable as such, it's already on its way to being over, and two because mimicking others leaves you failing to capitalize on your own unique talents and perspective.

Adaptable and Open

The *spirit* of polymathy is what's important, and it's largely independent of any particular fields, subjects, or topics, no matter how relevant they seem on the surface. It's about versatility, flexibility, and openness.

As an example, consider a person who believes that the future of clothing design and manufacture is changing, and that to survive they have to offer products that are ethically produced and appeal to more environmentally conscious buyers. Sounds good so far.

Such a person may find themselves working in fashion or textile buying, and try their best to build and market a new brand using all the old business principles that work for more traditional clothing manufacturers. But in their rigidity and dogged clinging to these methods, they may find themselves unwilling to change or learn something new, ignoring more subtle changes in the industry, failing to heed warnings that the "old ways" of doing things just won't work anymore.

Another person, a devoted polymath, may work in an entirely different field but simultaneously nurture a passion for buying and selling secondhand or vintage clothing. Though this person has zero business education and no experience, they have their finger on the true pulse of the fashion industry—renting and secondhand is the future. They act quickly and on inspiration, and within a year have established a thriving online clothing exchange platform that completely disrupts the market.

While the previous person is stalling in their career, the polymath achieves success with seemingly lightning speed and without following any of the rules. This is because their approach is not bound and limited by preconceptions, old models, possibly outdated beliefs and "business as usual" thinking.

Rather than this example being an anomaly, it's increasingly the norm: minimally trained and modestly experienced entrepreneurs frequently swoop in and succeed by virtue of their flexibility, creativity, and sometimes, sheer audacity. Here, mindset and attitude mean everything. This means being willing to adapt when necessary, to become comfortable and even expert at navigating quickly changing parameters and shifting challenges. A polymath typically doesn't react to adversity by asking what he can do to survive—*he is usually already doing it* when the opportunity rolls his way. Rather than reactive, survival-mode thinking, the polymath engages with ideas and topics long before everyone else, often simply because he enjoys doing so. This is why it's so important not to merely ape what polymaths *do*, but to closely examine the mindset and perspective that leads them to act that way when others are choosing differently.

Let's examine this attitude more closely. Firstly, a lesson any polymath can teach us is a healthy disregard for rules. Creative, inventive people see rules as provisional, and boundaries as mere working models until something better can be created or discovered. They know that right and wrong are often matters of (possibly flawed) opinion and don't let ordinary convention limit what they're willing to think about and imagine.

After all, engaging with material and ideas that are outside humanity's comfort zone requires you to suspend your ordinary judgments and assumptions. The inventor has an exuberance and curiosity that goes beyond what others may tell him is allowed or correct.

Going hand in hand with this attitude, necessarily, is an abiding comfort with uncertainty. For intelligent, creative people, there is a degree of responsibility associated with asking big questions and expecting answers.

Many historical polymaths held this attitude—"I didn't find the solution I wanted in the world, so I made it myself." This deep individuality and freedom comes from a willingness to tolerate the unknown, to act without complete information, to take risks and to live in a world that isn't already inhabited and charted by authorities who can tell you what you need to do.

Polymaths fail often, and sometimes extravagantly. They don't care—while others might think of unknowns and possible failures as intolerable, polymaths are not only able to march ahead, but to thrive in these conditions.

Without a sincere curiosity and love for developing authentic knowledge and mastery, people can seldom endure the process it takes to reach grand, long-term goals. But these are precisely the goals that most polymaths hold dear. They focus on what they want and don't allow anything to limit them—including their own irrational fears or laziness.

Finally, polymaths think of themselves in the same way they think of the various subjects they readily engage with—without the restriction and burden of boxes and oversimplified labels. When you think about it, so many of us are surprisingly ready to label ourselves one way or another, happy to take on the implied limitations. Polymaths don't bother; they seldom define themselves, and keep open to possibility and potential as long as possible.

Consider that today we have more labels for sexual identity and orientation than ever. You can choose which political party, personality type, blood group, demographic or social class you belong to, and place immense significance in these labels. There are labels for what religious beliefs you have or don't have, the sports teams you support, the nation you're part of, the race, even the media you consume and in what language. You can even take a DNA test to more precisely identify which ethnic groups you belong to.

The trouble with all this rampant labeling is that it closes you off to genuine, authentic, spontaneous engagement with life as it is, rather than life as someone-who-is-like-you sees it. For example, you tell yourself "I'm not an R&B person, I hate it to be honest" and completely forego listening to an artist you might have actually loved. Your identity here acted as a limitation, clearly separating what you felt was part of your world and what wasn't.

Polymaths, by setting these limitations far less often, allow themselves greater access to new realms. They don't care if a certain idea, behavior or question isn't for people like them, and they certainly aren't afraid to change their minds or question whether a previous preference is still useful. They are agnostic in their pursuit for an answer or a goal, and preconceptions, assumptions, and pride are put to the side.

This is a profound idea that bears repeating: our concept of ourselves informs the experiences and knowledge we are willing to expose ourselves to. It can even become a self-fulfilling prophecy: tell yourself often enough that you are a particular type of person, and you'll eventually take enough actions to support that claim that it will essentially be true. To get into the polymath mindset, ask yourself about the choices that you make, the opinions you have and the questions you ask—are you simply acting off of a preconceived idea of your identity? You vote, shop, speak and work like an ABC because you're an ABC and that's what ABCs do. However, people change. How will you know if you never allow for the possibility that one day you might do or want or feel something that goes against your old identity?

The key to rolling with change—and to being an adaptable, flexible polymath thinker—is to not cling too tightly to ideas of who we are and what our limits are. Are you the same person now that you were ten or twenty years ago? If not, you probably shouldn't behave as though the way you are now is the fixed, final form of your identity forevermore.

By being fluid and taking nothing for granted—not even the identity of the person who could take anything for granted—a polymath stays fresh and open to change, to new opportunities. They grow faster and with less disturbance, since they don't cling to old ideas that no longer work. They're not afraid to acknowledge when they've been wrong or abandon a project, even if they've invested considerably in it. For an intelligent, curious polymath, there is never an end-state where identity is fixed, all questions are answered, and life simply stands still. Of course, you want to uphold and honor your values. Yes, you have your preferences and your loves and your habits. But unlike others, you regularly subject those loves and preferences and habits to question, and constantly ask if something is working optimally, or if it can be better.

Polymaths don't waste time identifying as anyone in particular—they see their identities as whatever they need to be to help them do whatever it is they want to do. That's often why you see truly accomplished people shrinking away from others labeling them a "genius." This shows that their efforts are not about bolstering an ego or sense of identity—it's not about who they are, but what they do, what they know, and what they can learn.

Experimental

So, polymaths are open-minded, curious, and a little fearless. They can't be defined easily, and they like it that way. Another element of the polymath worldview that bears looking at is what can only be called an "experimental mindset." There's a reason so many famous polymaths throughout history have been involved in some way or another with the "hard sciences." There's something about the scientific method that captures and formalizes a polymath's natural curiosity. Scientific experiments asks questions such as:

"How does the world actually work? Why did this thing behave this way and not some other way? How can I look more closely at it?

What happens if I do this and what does this show me about this weird thing I'm trying to learn about?"

Though scientific thinking may come more naturally to some people than others, there are always ways to encourage and cultivate this ability. It only requires a subtle but important shift in thinking: don't just assume something, *test it out for real*. Everyone always says such-and-so is the case, but do you have evidence? You don't know how a new plan or idea will pan out—so why not test it?

Experimentation is something that's a little easier to understand in terms of actual physics or chemistry, but in reality, there are countless real-world benefits to conducting experiments in every area of life. One benefit is that, by thinking about practical implementation, you take any hypothetical "one day" ideas and force them into the present, without perfectionism preventing them from ever amounting to anything.

Waiting for the perfect time or perfect opportunity often means you never act or learn anything new—but if you just try something, test it out or give it a spin even though it's not perfect yet, you'll advance more than if you'd dawdled and procrastinated.

By conducting experiments, you give yourself access to what all scientists want: quality data. You can talk hypothetically for years and never have anything tangible to show for it. That's because trying things out *for real* gives you information you can actually use.

Experimentation offers you the opportunity to try something different, and see how it goes. When you frame your personal development, challenges or goals as experiments, you take the pressure off while simultaneously getting you acting sooner. Many of us live with so many unchallenged assumptions that we could be free of if only we gave ourselves the chance to test something better.

Experimentation is a window for change. When you try something different, you are saying to the world: "I'm open-minded and curious as to the outcome. This may lead to something new and better, who knows!"

Have you met older people who talk

wistfully about all the things they could have done in their youth but didn't? When you experiment, you don't wonder how things could have turned out—you do them, so you *know*. Consequently, you open up a whole new vista of choice and potential change for yourself.

The word "experiment" implies something formal, rigorous, and lab-based. But you can carry out informal experiments all the time, on your own terms. If you find yourself procrastinating, try on the curious polymath scientist's attitude for size: become curious, and commit only to testing something out. What would happen if you tried X or Y? It's not the end of the world— only a form of asking questions, when it comes down to it. Take up a new hobby or habit for thirty days. Eat something new even if you have a suspicion you won't like it. Say "yes" even though you're a bit apprehensive.

Kicking yourself out of mundane day-to-day life and ordinary ruts and habits with experiments means opening a little window wide enough to ask, *What if I did something different?* You might find yourself convinced after the experiment of a certain course of action's value, or prove to yourself what a bad idea it would have been without going all-in.

Seeing tangible results to a mini experiment gives you a sense of agency over your world. You can ask questions, get answers and feedback, and ask better questions next time round. In other words, you can grow and learn.

Finally, if you want to make the spirit of experimental thinking a reality in your life, you need to lay the groundwork to make that possible. How? By encouraging an open sense of safety around experimentation. You need to feel able to fail without disastrous consequences or pressures.

Like creativity, curiosity cannot thrive in a hostile or risky atmosphere. If you perceive threat, your mind is likely to dwell on an attitude of conservative survival rather than expansive exploring and generous creativity. If you want to follow the polymath example, make room in your life to play, to explore, to ask questions— without judgment from an inner critic or fears that you have to be perfect or else.

Start by changing your very definition of failure. It doesn't make sense to be squeamish about failure—in fact, expect that it will and does happen, and is merely par for the course.

Instead of thinking that failure is humiliating, or proof that you're doing something wrong or even worse, that *you're* wrong, frame it as a necessary part of learning and growing. Learn to respect failure as part of the process, rather than a distraction from it. The experimental mindset, above all else, is the commitment to forever being in experiment: you try something, you see the results, you adjust, you try again. Repeat until the day you die. What's more, when you can center passion, curiosity and resilience against change and "failure," something else starts to happen. Your mind slowly switches from the end point to the process itself. You begin to enjoy the path toward finding knowledge, not merely the prize of achievement at the end. What many polymaths do without being taught is focus on "process, not outcomes." They create for the joy of creating. Solve problems because they relish the experience of working through them.

With time, the diligent effort to think experimentally can be internalized and become a joyous flow in the moment—with you continually updating and reevaluating as you go. In other words, learning and evolving becomes second nature. You do it for fun! Focus on the process, and you almost aren't bothered by the outcome—even if it is considered a "failure." When you maintain an experimental, open-minded attitude, you always win, no matter what your outcomes.

Beginner

The mindset of a *beginner*—even to the point of considering yourself a novice or amateur in something you've been familiar with for years—is extremely beneficial in helping you view the world as a learning grounds to continually develop your self and embrace the need for mental flexibility. By definition, any beginner is experimenting with something new and is also attempting to be open-minded, no matter the motivation.

Polymaths might seem to be multifaceted experts, but there's a problem with that perspective. A common misconception about being an "expert"—even among experts—is that it implies you don't have to learn anything anymore. You've reached the fullest extent of knowledge possible in a given situation, and any suggestion that you could still learn more is almost insulting. You think—or feel—that you've already transcended all limitations and that there's nowhere to go but down.

However, ideally, there's not much difference between a beginner's mindset and an expert's. That's because when someone decides they want to become an expert on any subject, the first thing they have to accept is that they will *never stop learning* about that subject. Long after they've established themselves as an authority, they will still be learning and discovering just how much they still don't know. A true expert never stops wanting to fill in those gaps. The expert and the beginner therefore share an openness to new knowledge and insight.

The beginner's mindset is drawn from the Zen Buddhist concept *Shoshin*, described as "having an attitude of openness, eagerness, and lack of preconceptions when studying a subject, even when studying at an advanced level, just as a beginner in that subject would."

Every time you come across a new or even a familiar situation, no matter how shopworn or streetwise you think you are, reorient yourself to experiencing it as a beginner. Release all of your preconceived notions or expectations about the experience. Treat it with curiosity and a sense of wonder, as if you were seeing it for the first time.

As a quick illustration, imagine you see a herd of zebras outside of your bedroom window—hopefully a novel situation for you. Once you get over your initial shock, what are your initial observations and questions?

Does this situation remind you of something you're already familiar with or have seen in a movie, perhaps? You'd try to make sense of it all and construct a narrative to understand it. What happened beforehand, and what will happen after? What details are surprising or downright odd when you think beyond first glance? You'd certainly focus on questions of "why" and "how." You would probably also be overwhelmed with sensation and stimuli. You'd have many more questions than answers, and you'd be fixated on trying to figure out the logistics and probabilities of such an occasion.

In other words, you're approaching this herd of zebras with a sense of wonder and openness. On the other hand, looking outside and seeing an errant bird or squirrel certainly won't evoke the same sense of interest or curiosity.

Now let's take another example of learning how to play a new instrument. What questions would you ask? Where would you even start? You wouldn't know what is and isn't important, so everything would seem significant at first. You'd probably be curious as to the limits of the instrument— first in how to not break it, and then in its overall capabilities. You'd be filled with wonder and also caution for fear of making an error or breaking it. Again, you'd have so many questions, and the answers you receive wouldn't begin to scratch the surface. You won't forget the immediate impression the instrument makes on you for a very long time.

Those are the underpinnings of the beginner mindset. When you reprogram your mind to a blank slate and act as if you truly have no knowledge about something, you'll engage in extensive, curious questioning, and knowledge will come far easier than in acting like you already have the answers.

It should be emphasized that the polymath beginner's mindset empowers the ability to ask *dumb questions*. So-called experts rely on assumptions and their own experiences, often without further investigation. When you feel comfortable asking *dumb questions*, nothing is left up to assumptions and chance, and everything is out in the open and clarified. Experts and polymaths can sometimes have blind spots because of patterns they're familiar with from other fields, but those may not always apply in novel situations.

You can approach both new *and* familiar situations with this same principle. Next time you're driving a car, try noticing the things you would automatically do otherwise and say them out loud to yourself. Along with that, focus on what you sense when you're behind the wheel but have long since stopped paying attention to: the ridges in the steering wheel, the glow of the dashboard odometer, or the sound of the air-conditioner. Even these crushingly insignificant details could unlock and reveal some new element or impression that you've never experienced before.

Overall, the beginner's mindset requires slowing down, setting aside preconceived notions, and paying attention to what you've ignored for a long time.

Belief

Belief may seem simplistic, but it is not something that everyone possesses.

Polymaths, whether through sheer belief or ignorance of the obstacles in their way, believe that with time, effort, and energy, they will eventually reach their solution or goal. Often this journey will involve gaining depth of knowledge and becoming the proverbial pi-shape. And with learning, improving, or achieving any goal, whether you believe you can or cannot, you will end up being correct.

To illustrate, we turn to British runner Sir Roger Bannister. The name Roger Bannister may not be familiar to you unless you're a track and field fan or a historian of athletics.

In 1954, Roger Bannister was the first man to break the four-minute barrier for the mile, a longstanding threshold that athletes had flirted with constantly but had never crossed.

One complete mile is four laps around a standard track. This means to break the four-minute threshold, a runner would need a pace of, at most, sixty seconds per lap—something that was thought to be impossible. The whole idea that a human being could run a mile in under four minutes was considered a fantasy, and even track experts predicted that humans would never achieve it. You have to remember that this was decades ago, when modern competitive athletics were still in their nascent stage—nothing close to the training, nutrition, or attention we give them today. These athletes were competing using methods that are absolutely prehistoric in comparison to modern techniques.

The world record for the mile was stalled around 4:02 and 4:01 for over a decade, so there seemed to be some truth to the belief that humans had finally reached their physical potential. It had been lowered steadily up to that point, starting from the first modern Olympics in 1896, when the gold medalist of the 1,500 meters won in a time of 4:33, which is the rough equivalent of a 4:46 mile.

We had come so far, there had to be a limit, and we seemed to have hit it. Of course, similar notions of limits of human capabilities have existed in more modern times, such as the ten-second barrier for the 100-meter dash. For comparison's sake, the world record for the mile as of 2020 is 3:43.13, held by Hicham El Guerrouj of Morocco.

At the 1952 Helsinki Summer Olympics, Bannister finished in fourth place in the 1,500-meter run (the *metric* mile), just short of receiving a medal. Motivated by his disappointment and shame, he set his sights on running a sub-four-minute mile, which he felt would exonerate him. Bannister, unlike all other runners and experts at the time, believed that it was possible, so he trained with that in mind. It was a matter of *when*, not *if*, for him. Just making the assumption that something is a certainty, and even planning for what happens when you surpass it, can force you to behave in a drastically different manner than you otherwise would.

All the while a doctor-in-training, Bannister began in earnest to attempt breaking the threshold in 1954. He accomplished the feat on May 6 by 0.6 seconds in a time of 3:59.4. People were in disbelief, and he was revered as superhuman. For his efforts, he was knighted in 1975 and enjoyed a long life representing British athletic interests both domestically and internationally. Again, he accomplished this all while he was a practicing doctor and neurologist.

Here's where belief truly comes into the story of Sir Roger Bannister and the four-minute mile. Within two months of his breaking the four-minute mark, an Australian runner named John Landy broke both the four-minute mark *and* Bannister's world record. The following year, three other runners also broke the four-minute mark. The next decade saw over a dozen people cross the four-minute mark that had stymied runners for years.

Such is the power of belief. People have preconceptions about what is possible and what is out of their reach. But most of the time, these ideas simply limit them. They allow themselves to be disenfranchised by what they perceive to be possible or not, what they perceive they are capable of or not, and what they believe they can and can't be.

Without belief, you are putting an arbitrary limit on yourself. You sabotage yourself and may never even get started.

In the months following Bannister's achievement, nothing about those other four runners changed physically. They didn't magically grow winged feet or use performance-enhancing drugs as today's athletes might. They didn't alter their training habits or regimens. All that conceivably could have changed was their mindset of belief: they were certain the four-minute threshold could be beaten, and they were going to do it! That was the only element that shifted.

Roger Bannister redefined what was possible and instilled others with belief. If Bannister had lacked belief that his goal was achievable, he would have been happy with a time of 4:01 and then lived with regret for the rest of his life when someone else like John Landy came along and was first to break the tape in under four minutes.

Polymaths believe they can become experts, they believe they can excel, and they believe that what they wish to achieve is within reach—in fact, it is just *out of reach*, which keeps them powerfully motivated and striving for more. They believe that obstacles can be overcome, and that they can persevere no matter how tough those barriers are. They believe that failure and struggle are pitstops along the way.

This brings us to our last element of the polymathic mind: perseverance.

Relentless

Ultimately, in order to become true polymaths, we will have to push beyond what we like, enjoy, and feel comfortable with. That's the nature of achieving larger goals. At the core, we still need to engage in something we find at least slightly annoying or uncomfortable.

In other words, there are no shortcuts, no easy life hacks, no quick tricks. Success in the bigger picture belongs to those who have mastered the ability to tolerate a degree of distress and uncertainty and who can thrive in situations of sacrifice in service of something bigger than their immediate pleasure in the moment.

The road to polymathy = being uncomfortable.

We all want to grow and achieve, but the state of growth is inherently an uncomfortable one. Evolving feels uncertain and risky at times, and it certainly requires us to give up immediate pleasures and old, easy habits. Growth and development is about expanding, risking, exploring. It cannot be done without leaving the security of the old behind. And sometimes, change requires pain, as the old dies and the new is still small and uncertain.

Self-discipline is not required for the easy parts of life. It takes no effort or special technique to enjoy what we already enjoy. But if we want to productively approach the rest of life, we need to develop the self-discipline to work with the things we don't enjoy. Rather than thinking of pain, discomfort, and uncertainty as roadblocks in our way to pleasure and success, we understand that they're simply a part of life, and if we manage them well, we can unlock even bigger pleasures.

There is a great paradox in learning to not just tolerate but embrace discomfort. Practicing being uncomfortable doesn't sound like much fun, and it isn't. But it is a skill that will reap far more rewards in the long term than merely chasing fleeting pleasures or shifting fancies in each moment.

Simply, we practice self-discipline and familiarity with discomfort because we respect that life contains an inevitable amount of unpleasant feelings. We know that in gaining a new perspective on the things we don't really want to do, we actually create new opportunities for fulfillment, meaning, and pleasure. Life becomes easier, and we become stronger, almost larger than the everyday trials and troubles the world can throw our way.

With self-discipline, our expectations become healthier and more in line with reality. Our work becomes more focused and purposeful and we are able to achieve more. Self-discipline is not a thing we simply decide we want or think is a good idea in theory. It's a practice that we pitch up for again and again, every day and every moment, willing to work it out in the arena of our lived experience. In other words, self-discipline is a habit in a world where the easiest thing is to take the path of least resistance or fall prey to the "succeed without trying" traps all around us.

It might seem logical at first to pursue pleasure—if it feels good, it must be good, right? But if there's one thing we know with utmost certainty, it's that things *will* change around us, we *will* have to endure suffering at one point or another, and we *will* be uncomfortable and forced to face things we wish we didn't have to. If we have this knowledge, isn't it better to be prepared rather than blindly pursue a dazzling goal with no thought to what you'll do when that goal doesn't go how you planned?

Learning how to tolerate distress, uncertainty, doubt, and risk while things are okay (i.e., before these things are forced on you) gives you the opportunity to practice and develop your discipline so you're prepared for future discomfort. Yes, it means that walking barefoot makes you more "immune" to one day having to walk without shoes. But it also means you're less attached to needing shoes, and you feel deep down that you are more than able to respond to and endure challenges. This is an attitude of empowerment. It's looking at life's challenges head-on and deciding to accept them and respond with dignity and grit.

Practicing tolerance is a "vaccine" in that you inoculate yourself against future discomfort in general. Adversity will still bother you, but you'll move through it with the quiet confidence that it won't kill you. How can it, when you've endured it all before and only came out stronger?

You can turn your focus to maximizing pleasure and refusing to engage with pain; or you can acknowledge that life intends to serve you heaping doses of both, and if you can prepare with maturity and wisdom, you can stay calm and ride those waves, trusting that you've developed your ability to thrive.

So prepare while the going is still easy. Don't wait for life to force you to learn the lessons you must. Take the initiative by developing self-discipline right now. The shift is only a small one, but it has great influence on how you approach yourself and life. The idea is straightforward: get more uncomfortable than you'd usually be. Give yourself the gift of the opportunity to grow stronger.

Here is a brief passage from *Meditations* by the Roman emperor-philosopher Marcus Aurelius that illustrates what we lose by surrendering to discomfort and not taking steps toward what we want in life:

> "At dawn, when you have trouble getting out of bed, tell yourself: 'I have to go to work—as a human being. What do I have to complain of, if I'm going to do what I was born for—the things I was brought into the world to do? Or is this what I was created for? To huddle under the blankets and stay warm?'
>
> 'But it's nicer here...'
>
> So you were born to feel 'nice'? Instead of doing things and experiencing them? Don't you see the plants, the birds, the ants and spiders and bees

going about their individual tasks, putting the world in order, as best they can? And you're not willing to do your job as a human being? Why aren't you running to do what your nature demands?

'—But we have to sleep sometime...'

Agreed. But nature set a limit on that—as it did on eating and drinking. And you're over the limit. You've had more than enough of that. But not of working. There you're still below your quota. You don't love yourself enough. Or you'd love your nature too, and what it demands of you. People who love what they do wear themselves down doing it, they even forget to wash or eat."

Polymaths are people who, as Marcus Aurelius says, "love what they do"—and they're willing to put up with discomfort when, in the long run, doing so allows them to achieve their goals and lead a fulfilling life.

Takeaways:

- The set of knowledge that a polymath has may differ completely from another polymath, but at their cores, they are extremely similar. This is because of the drive, curiosity, and openness required to become pi or comb-shaped, as opposed to just T-shaped. For instance, do you think that someone like Leonardo da Vinci looked at a problem he was unfamiliar with and said, "Someone else will take care of that, I'm going to take a nap"? Probably not.

- The first mental trait of polymaths is extreme adaptability and openness. Whatever the obstacle, it can be navigated or circumvented. It can be solved. To achieve this, you must embody flexible and resourceful thinking, and not be bound by convention or personal habit. You must be open to new perspectives and the unfamiliar and novel. For instance, who was the first person to look at a cow's udders and think that they should drink what comes out?

- Second, polymaths live experimentally. This isn't to say that they are always conducting traditional scientific experiments; rather, they're applying the scientific method by analyzing and investigating whatever they come across. They feel safe doing this and simply want to gain new information and sate their curiosity. It's almost like they cannot stop themselves from doing it.

- Third, polymaths embody the beginner mindset, which is actually far more useful than the expert mindset. When you're a beginner, you have ten times more questions than answers. And that's a good thing. It makes you listen and question and dig deeper. Experts all too often fall into the trap of assuming they know too much, which inevitably causes blind spots. The beginner mindset should be applied in combination with critical thinking, and together they create a worthy line of inquiry.

- Fourth, polymaths have belief in themselves. Whether it is well-placed or delusional, they believe that they will reach their goal. Many people are their own worst enemies when it comes to learning. But this speaks to something even more fundamental: the belief of agency, or ability to act and achieve. This means that output equals input, within reasonable expectations. One cannot reach a goal if they don't believe they are capable of it first.

- Finally, polymaths can be described as relentless. How else would you describe people with deep knowledge in multiple realms? Being relentless can be defined as overcoming obstacles and discomfort at all costs. And yet often, the only true cost is simply being uncomfortable. Polymaths have the utmost self-discipline because starting from ground zero, even if you are interested in a topic, is difficult, tiring, and can cause mass confusion. But that's life. And being comfortable with this uncertainty is a skill that makes you relentless toward getting to point B.

CHAPTER 1. DECONSTRUCTING THE POLYMATH

- We're often told in different ways that the key to success is specialization, and that being a generalist is inadvisable. Yet, many of the smartest individuals that have ever graced the earth are renowned for being polymaths with skills across multiple subjects.
- The modern workplace and companies are increasingly reliant on polymathic individuals to bring them success, making it imperative for us to diversify our skill set instead of simply mastering one trade and sticking to it.
- But what exactly is a polymath? Howard Gardner's theory of multiple intelligences might be useful in answering this question. He lays out

seven different intelligences that include musical, spatial, linguistic, and other abilities that we all possess. A polymath is simply someone who has developed three or more of these intelligences.

- Alternatively, we have the biological view of polymathy. According to this perspective, different parts of our brain are responsible for their own unique functions. Our ability to write is dictated by one part of our cerebrum, while the capacity to comprehend writing is controlled by another part. A polymath is someone with an exceptionally developed brain whose cerebral lobes have matured beyond the average.

- So which of the two is accurate? The truth is that both of these theories are highly flawed and unsupported by any kind of scientific research. Gardner's multiple intelligences is simply a theory that can't be proved scientifically, while the idea that specific parts of our brain alone conduct certain functions is patently false.

- A true polymath is someone who possesses three components of knowledge: breadth, depth, and integration. This is also known as cross-pollination. Such a person has acquired expertise in at least a few different domains, and can successfully integrate those domains together instead of treating them as unrelated and distinct subjects or skills. So a scientist who is also artistically inclined can use the latter to aid his research in ways that will make him more successful than the average member of his field.

CHAPTER 2. HOW TO INCREASE LEARNING AND SKILL TRANSFER

- While you're learning to be a polymath, perhaps the most difficult task you'll face is to integrate your knowledge from different disciplines. The concept of *learning transfer* will make this part of achieving polymathy significantly simpler.

- A learning transfer occurs when you use knowledge or skills acquired in a certain context in an area that is different from the original one. There are several types of learning transfers. Among these are positive and negative transfers. The former is simply a successful learning transfer, whereas a negative transfer occurs when knowledge acquired in one context hinders learning in another. Then there are simple and complex transfers. Simple transfers occur when you transfer learning from one context to another one that is similar to the first, whereas complex transfers involve transference to more disparate contexts. Finally, there are also specific and non-specific transfers. When the context to which you're transferring your knowledge has clear similarities with the original one, a specific transfer occurs. However, when there are no apparent similarities between the two contexts, a non-specific transfer occurs.

- There are several science-backed tips you can follow to improve the chances of a positive transfer. Generally, those who are enthusiastic about their learning and are often to apply it to different settings are more successful at transferring it to other contexts. It has also been shown that people who are optimistic and confident about their ability to transfer their learning are more able to do so.

- In addition to these tips, there are some guidelines you can follow to maximize your ability to transfer your learning. Primary among these is learning the concept of metacognition, which is the process of being able to think about your thinking, and use that to regulate your thought and learning process by asking yourself questions. Besides this, practice transference in different contexts, far and near, use different types of media while learning, and keep looking for connections between what you've learned and unrelated contexts.

- Problem-based learning is where you deliberately choose a problem to solve, or a goal to achieve, which will necessitate the learning of a skill. In essence, instead of setting out to learn X, the idea is to set a goal of solving problem Y, and in the process, learn X. This will keep you engaged and motivated, and also drive deeper learning because you will take ownership of something and put all the pieces together yourself. For instance, you will need to identify what you know, what you don't know, identify solutions, and take action.

CHAPTER 3. BREAKING KNOWLEDGE DOWN

- When you encounter new information from sources that you're unfamiliar with, some of it will undoubtedly be complex and inaccessible. This can often serve as an incentive for people to abandon their quest for polymathy. However, analogies are an extremely powerful tool that makes breaking down complicated information easy and efficient.

- Analogies are essentially comparisons between two seemingly unrelated concepts or skills. To maximize your learning, you'll need to learn how to use what you already know and draw connections to what you're learning in innovative ways. This forces you to transfer your learning, ensuring you retain more information in the long-term.

- To start using analogies for learning, you'll need to familiarize yourself with academic analogies. These consists of four parts divided into two groups. On the left side, you make a certain type of connection between things you know about, like code in video games. Code is the main building block upon which video games are built. If you're learning law, you'll know that law is to constitution what code is to video games. To use the standard analogy format, we'd state this as: "code : video games :: law : constitution."

- The kind of connection you make on the left side of your analogy varies drastically depending on the type of analogy you use. The two can be synonyms, antonyms, have a part-whole relationship, etc. While learning, you'll need to decide which types fit your topic best, and use as many of them as possible.

- Once you're comfortable with drawing analogies, you can also follow some simple steps to make sure you get the most out of them. Try to refrain from using analogies for simple concepts and reserve them only for difficult ones to avoid confusion. Use plenty of concrete examples to simplify abstract concepts and information. Additionally, you should review the purpose of your analogy from time to time, since it can be easy to remember the comparison but difficult to recall what made it an accurate one.

- One technique that compliments analogies exquisitely is mind mapping. This tool draws connections between different concepts within the same topic to keep track of how they all connect to each other. The most basic way to create a mind map is to start with a circle in the middle of some paper and draw branches that extend from it. Fill these branch-endings with sub-topics and extend even more branches to exhaust the sub-topic. You can use this method to keep track of all your analogies, while also adding additional information relevant to them.

CHAPTER 4. THE POLYMATHIC MIND

- The set of knowledge that a polymath has may differ completely from another polymath, but at their cores, they are extremely similar. This is because of the drive, curiosity, and openness required to become pi or comb-shaped, as opposed to just T-shaped. For instance, do you think that someone like Leonardo da Vinci looked at a problem he was unfamiliar with and said, "Someone else will take care of that, I'm going to take a nap"? Probably not.

- The first mental trait of polymaths is extreme adaptability and openness. Whatever the obstacle, it can be navigated or circumvented. It can be solved. To achieve this, you must embody flexible and resourceful thinking, and not be bound by convention or personal habit. You must be open to new perspectives and the unfamiliar and novel. For instance, who was the first person to look at a cow's udders and think that they should drink what comes out?

- Second, polymaths live experimentally. This isn't to say that they are always conducting traditional scientific experiments; rather, they're applying the scientific method by analyzing and investigating whatever they come across. They feel safe doing this and simply want to gain new information and sate their curiosity. It's almost like they cannot stop themselves from doing it.

- Third, polymaths embody the beginner mindset, which is actually far more useful than the expert mindset. When you're a beginner, you have ten times more questions than answers. And that's a good thing. It makes you listen and question and dig deeper. Experts all too often fall into the trap of assuming they know too much, which inevitably causes blind spots. The beginner mindset should be applied in combination with critical thinking, and together they create a worthy line of inquiry.

- Fourth, polymaths have belief in themselves. Whether it is well-placed or delusional, they believe that they will reach their goal. Many people are their own worst enemies when it comes to learning. But this speaks to something even more fundamental: the belief of agency, or ability to act and achieve. This means that output equals input, within reasonable expectations. One cannot reach a goal if they don't believe they are capable of it first.

- Finally, polymaths can be described as relentless. How else would you describe people with deep knowledge in multiple realms? Being relentless can be defined as overcoming obstacles and discomfort at all costs. And yet often, the only true cost is simply being uncomfortable. Polymaths have the utmost self-discipline because starting from ground zero, even if you are interested in a topic, is difficult, tiring, and can cause mass confusion. But that's life. And being comfortable with this uncertainty is a skill that makes you relentless toward getting to point B.